MANAGING PROJECTS IN TOXIC ENVIRONMENTS

TEAM MANAGEMENT | CHALLENGING ENVIRONMENTS | MANAGING PROJECTS IN TOXIC ENVIRONMENTS

ANGELA SIRBU, MBA. PMP

© 2024 by Angela Sirbu, MBA. PMP. All rights reserved.

No part of this book may be reproduced or utilized in any form or by any means, electronic or mechanical, including photocopying, recording, or by any information storage and retrieval system, without permission in writing from the publisher.

First Edition 2024

Published by Angela Sirbu, MBA. PMP

CONTENTS

INTRODUCTION

CHAPTER 1: UNDERSTANDING TOXIC ENVIRONMENTS

CHAPTER 2: BUILDING RESILIENCE IN PROJECT TEAMS

CHAPTER 3: EFFECTIVE LEADERSHIP STYLES FOR TOXIC ENVIRONMENTS

CHAPTER 4: CONFLICT RESOLUTION STRATEGIES

CHAPTER 5: MAINTAINING TEAM MORALE

CHAPTER 6: COMMUNICATION TACTICS FOR TOXIC ENVIRONMENTS

CHAPTER 7: RISK MANAGEMENT IN ADVERSE CONDITIONS

CHAPTER 8: ENHANCING PRODUCTIVITY DESPITE CHALLENGES

CHAPTER 9: LEVERAGING DIVERSITY IN TOXIC ENVIRONMENTS

CHAPTER 10: CASE STUDIES OF SUCCESS IN TOXIC ENVIRONMENTS

CHAPTER 11: TOOLS AND TECHNIQUES FOR MANAGING TOXICITY

CHAPTER 12: LEGAL AND ETHICAL CONSIDERATIONS

CHAPTER 13: CREATING A SUSTAINABLE POSITIVE ENVIRONMENT

INTRODUCTION

In the dynamic world of project management, professionals often find themselves navigating not only the complexities of tasks and timelines but also the intricate web of human interactions and organizational cultures. "Managing Projects in Toxic Environments" delves into this multifaceted challenge, offering insights and strategies for steering projects to success amid adverse conditions. Toxic environments can manifest in various forms, from dysfunctional teams and corrosive workplace politics to inefficient processes and lack of leadership support. Such conditions can significantly hinder progress, morale, and the overall success of a project.

This book serves as a comprehensive guide for project managers, team leaders, and stakeholders who must operate in less-than-ideal settings. It sheds light on the nuanced dynamics of toxic work environments and provides practical tools to manage and mitigate their impacts. Through a combination of theoretical frameworks, real-world case studies, and actionable advice, readers will gain a deeper understanding of how to identify toxic elements, foster resilience, and build a cohesive team capable of overcoming adversity.

Effective project management in challenging environments requires a unique blend of technical acumen, emotional intelligence, and strategic foresight. This book emphasizes the importance of clear communication, adaptive leadership, and the cultivation of a positive work culture, even when external circumstances are far from optimal. By addressing both the human and procedural aspects of project management, it equips readers with the skills needed to turn potential obstacles into opportunities for growth and innovation.

"Managing Projects in Toxic Environments" is not just a manual for survival; it is a roadmap for thriving in the face of adversity. It empowers readers to transform toxic scenarios into productive and rewarding experiences, ensuring that projects are not only completed but also leave a lasting positive impact on the teams and organizations involved.

Chapter 1: Understanding Toxic Environments

Defining Toxicity in the Workplace

Toxicity in the workplace can be likened to an invisible gas that permeates every corner, affecting morale, productivity, and overall well-being. It may not be immediately visible but its effects are deeply felt. The signs of a toxic work environment often manifest through a spectrum of behaviors and atmospheres that can make even the most dedicated employees feel drained and disengaged. Understanding these signs is crucial in managing projects in such environments.

One of the most glaring indicators of toxicity is poor communication. This goes beyond mere misunderstandings or occasional lapses in information sharing. In a toxic workplace, communication is often laced with negativity, sarcasm, and passive-aggressive undertones. Constructive feedback is replaced with harsh criticism, and important information is frequently withheld as a means of control or manipulation. This breakdown in communication erodes trust and fosters an atmosphere of suspicion and resentment.

Another hallmark of a toxic environment is the prevalence of cliques and favoritism. In such settings, certain groups or individuals are given preferential treatment while others are marginalized or ignored. This creates a divisive atmosphere where collaboration is stifled, and employees are pitted against one another. The resulting competition is not healthy or productive; instead, it breeds hostility and undermines teamwork.

Excessive stress and burnout are also telltale signs of workplace toxicity. When employees are consistently overwhelmed with unrealistic deadlines, excessive workloads, and a lack of support, it leads to chronic stress. Over time, this can result in burnout, characterized by emotional exhaustion, cynicism, and a decline in professional efficacy. A toxic work environment often fails to recognize or address these issues, instead perpetuating a cycle of high demands and low support.

The presence of bullying and harassment is another critical aspect of toxicity. This can take many forms, from overt aggression and intimidation to more subtle forms of psychological manipulation. Regardless of its manifestation, bullying creates a climate of fear and anxiety, making it difficult for employees to perform their duties effectively. It also contributes to a pervasive sense of insecurity and instability within the workplace.

Micromanagement is a further symptom of a toxic work environment. When managers excessively control and scrutinize every detail of their employees' work, it stifles creativity and innovation. Employees feel undervalued and distrusted, leading to decreased motivation and engagement. This type of management style often results in high turnover rates, as employees seek out more supportive and empowering work environments.

Moreover, a lack of recognition and appreciation can significantly contribute to workplace toxicity. When employees' efforts and achievements go unnoticed or unacknowledged, it diminishes their sense of value and purpose. This lack of recognition can lead to disengagement and a decline in overall morale, as employees feel that their hard work is not appreciated or rewarded.

In addition to these factors, a toxic workplace is often characterized by a lack of transparency and accountability. Decisions are made behind closed doors, and there is little to no explanation provided for changes or directives. This opacity breeds confusion and mistrust, as employees are left in the dark about the reasoning behind important decisions. Furthermore, when mistakes are made, there is often a reluctance to take responsibility, with blame being shifted or deflected.

Understanding these various elements that define toxicity in the workplace is essential for effectively managing projects in such environments. Recognizing the signs and their detrimental impact on employees and organizational health is the first step towards addressing and mitigating the negative effects of a toxic workplace.

Identifying Key Toxic Behaviors

Navigating through a project in a toxic environment requires a keen eye for identifying the specific behaviors that contribute to such a detrimental atmosphere. These behaviors, often subtle yet profoundly impactful, can derail the most well-planned projects and demoralize even the most resilient teams. Recognizing these key toxic behaviors is the first step in mitigating their effects and steering the project back on course.

One of the most prevalent toxic behaviors is chronic negativity. This manifests as a persistent pessimism that permeates the team, with individuals constantly highlighting problems without offering solutions. This behavior can be particularly insidious as it saps motivation and fosters a culture of defeatism. Team members may become reluctant to share ideas or take initiative, fearing their contributions will be met with criticism or dismissal.

Micromanagement is another toxic behavior that can stifle a project. When leaders excessively control every aspect of their team's work, it can lead to a significant decrease in creativity and innovation. Team members may feel undervalued and distrusted, which can result in decreased morale and productivity. Instead of empowering individuals to leverage their unique skills and perspectives, micromanagement creates an environment of dependency and anxiety.

Blame-shifting is a behavior that can quickly erode trust within a team. When individuals or leaders consistently deflect responsibility and point fingers at others, it creates a climate of fear and defensiveness. Team members may become preoccupied with protecting themselves rather than focusing on collaborative problem-solving. This behavior undermines accountability and can lead to a toxic culture where mistakes are hidden rather than addressed constructively.

Gossip and exclusionary practices are also significant contributors to a toxic project environment. When team members engage in backchannel conversations and form cliques, it can lead to feelings of isolation and insecurity among those who are excluded. This behavior disrupts team cohesion and can create an atmosphere of suspicion and hostility. Effective communication and inclusivity are essential for maintaining a healthy team dynamic, and gossip undermines both.

Passive-aggressive behavior is another subtle yet damaging toxic trait. This can include indirect resistance to tasks, procrastination, and a lack of communication. Team members exhibiting passive-aggressive behavior may agree to tasks verbally but fail to follow through, creating confusion and delays. This behavior can be challenging to address as it often flies under the radar, but its impact on team efficiency and morale can be significant.

Lastly, a lack of transparency from leadership can foster a toxic environment. When leaders withhold information or fail to communicate openly with their team, it can lead to uncertainty and mistrust. Team members may feel they are being kept in the dark, which can result in disengagement and a lack of commitment to the project's goals. Transparent communication is crucial for building trust and ensuring that everyone is aligned and informed.

Identifying these toxic behaviors is crucial for any project manager aiming to foster a healthy, productive working environment. By recognizing and addressing these behaviors early, it's possible to mitigate their impact and set the stage for a more collaborative and successful project.

The Impact of Toxic Environments on Projects

Navigating the murky waters of project management in toxic environments is akin to steering a ship through a tumultuous storm. The adverse conditions these environments create can have profound effects on the trajectory and outcome of any project. Toxicity in the workplace manifests in various forms, including poor communication, lack of trust, pervasive negativity, and unproductive conflict. These elements collectively erode the foundational pillars of successful project management.

The first casualty in a toxic environment is often communication. Clear, open channels of communication are essential for any project's success. In a toxic setting, however, communication tends to become fragmented, guarded, and often misleading. Team members may withhold crucial information due to fear of retribution or a lack of trust in their colleagues. This breakdown not only delays the project timeline but also leads to a series of misunderstandings and errors that can be detrimental to the project's integrity.

Trust, the cornerstone of any collaborative effort, is another victim. In environments where backstabbing, blame games, and favoritism are rampant, trust becomes a scarce commodity. Team members are less likely to collaborate effectively when they are suspicious of each other's motives. This distrust breeds a culture of isolation, where individuals focus more on self-preservation rather than the collective goal. Such a climate makes it nearly impossible to foster the kind of teamwork and synergy that are vital for project success.

Negativity acts as a slow poison, seeping into every aspect of the project. A negative atmosphere can sap the enthusiasm and motivation out of even the most dedicated team members. When the general mood is one of pessimism and defeatism, it becomes challenging to maintain momentum. The lack of morale can lead to increased absenteeism, lower productivity, and a higher turnover rate, all of which are detrimental to the project's progress.

Conflict, while inevitable in any group setting, takes on a more destructive nature in toxic environments. Instead of being a source of growth and innovation, conflict in such settings often turns unproductive and personal. The focus shifts from resolving issues to winning arguments, leading to a hostile work environment. This not only hampers decision-making processes but also creates a breeding ground for resentment and grudges, which can linger and fester, further derailing the project.

Moreover, the ripple effects of working in a toxic environment extend beyond the immediate project team. Stakeholders, clients, and other external parties can sense the dysfunction, which can damage the organization's reputation and credibility. Trust and confidence in the organization's ability to deliver can be severely undermined, leading to a loss of business opportunities and partnerships.

The psychological toll on team members cannot be overlooked. The constant stress and anxiety of working in a toxic environment can lead to burnout, mental health issues, and a general sense of dissatisfaction. This not only affects their performance on the current project but can also have long-term implications for their careers and personal lives.

Addressing the impact of toxic environments on projects requires a multifaceted approach. It involves not just recognizing and mitigating the toxic elements but also fostering a culture of open communication, trust, positivity, and constructive conflict resolution. Only then can projects hope to thrive and achieve their desired outcomes in the face of adversity.

Initial Steps to Assess Toxicity

When stepping into a potentially toxic project environment, the first critical task is to assess the toxicity level accurately. This assessment involves a series of deliberate and systematic steps designed to gather comprehensive information, which will inform the subsequent management strategies. The initial phase is akin to a diagnostic procedure, where the goal is to identify the sources and symptoms of toxicity within the project.

Begin with a thorough review of the project's historical data and documentation. This includes examining past project reports, meeting minutes, and communication logs. Look for patterns of issues, recurring problems, and any previously identified risks. This historical context provides a foundation for understanding the current state of the project and highlights any long-standing issues that may have contributed to the toxic environment.

Next, engage in direct observation and interaction with the project team. Spend time in meetings, observe daily operations, and note the dynamics between team members. Pay attention to both verbal and non-verbal communication cues. Are team members openly communicating, or is there a noticeable tension? Are meetings productive, or do they devolve into unproductive conflict? These observations can reveal much about the underlying issues affecting the project.

Conduct one-on-one interviews with key stakeholders, including team members, project sponsors, and clients. These interviews should be structured yet open-ended, allowing for candid feedback. Ask about their perceptions of the project's progress, the challenges they face, and their views on team dynamics. Listen actively and take note of any recurring themes or concerns. This qualitative data is invaluable in painting a detailed picture of the project's health.

Utilize surveys and questionnaires to gather anonymous feedback from the broader project team. These tools can provide quantitative data on team morale, communication effectiveness, and perceived obstacles. Ensure that the surveys are designed to protect anonymity, encouraging honesty and reducing fear of reprisal. Analyze the results to identify common issues and areas of concern that might not be immediately visible through direct observation or interviews.

Assess the organizational culture and its impact on the project. Consider the alignment between the project's objectives and the organization's values and practices. A misalignment can often be a root cause of toxicity. Evaluate the support structures in place for the project team, such as training programs, resource availability, and leadership support. A lack of adequate support can exacerbate stress and contribute to a toxic environment.

Examine the project's governance and decision-making processes. Identify any bottlenecks or inefficiencies that may be causing frustration or delays. Assess the clarity and effectiveness of the project's communication channels. Poor communication is a common contributor to project toxicity, leading to misunderstandings and conflict.

Document all findings meticulously, creating a comprehensive toxicity assessment report. This report should detail the identified sources of toxicity, the symptoms observed, and the potential impact on the project's success. Include both qualitative and quantitative data to provide a holistic view of the project environment.

Share the assessment report with key stakeholders and discuss the findings openly. This transparency is crucial in building trust and fostering a collaborative approach to addressing the issues. Use the report as a basis for developing targeted interventions aimed at mitigating the identified sources of toxicity.

The initial steps to assess toxicity are fundamental in diagnosing the health of a project. A thorough and systematic approach not only uncovers the root causes of toxicity but also sets the stage for effective management and remediation strategies.

Chapter 2: Building Resilience in Project Teams

Fostering Emotional Intelligence

Navigating the murky waters of a toxic work environment can feel like a Herculean task, especially when managing projects that demand precision, collaboration, and unwavering focus. The undercurrents of negativity, mistrust, and tension can erode team morale and productivity. To steer the ship through such turbulent seas, one must harness the power of emotional intelligence, a critical skill that not only aids in personal resilience but also fosters a healthier, more cooperative team dynamic.

Emotional intelligence begins with self-awareness. Recognizing one's own emotions, strengths, and weaknesses is the first step toward managing them effectively. In a toxic environment, self-awareness allows a project manager to identify stress triggers and emotional responses that may cloud judgment or escalate conflicts. By maintaining a clear understanding of their emotional state, managers can remain calm and composed, setting a tone of stability and rationality for the team.

The next pillar, self-regulation, involves controlling or redirecting disruptive emotions and impulses. It's about staying in control, especially when faced with the provocations and pressures inherent in a toxic workplace. A project manager who can self-regulate will respond to challenging situations with thoughtful actions rather than reactive outbursts. This ability not only preserves their own mental well-being but also models positive behavior for the team, encouraging a culture of patience and thoughtful communication.

Motivation, another key component, drives individuals to achieve goals with energy and persistence. In a toxic environment, it can be all too easy to succumb to the pervasive negativity. However, a project manager with high emotional intelligence can tap into intrinsic motivation, keeping their focus on the broader objectives and the satisfaction of accomplishing them. By maintaining a positive outlook and demonstrating a commitment to the project's success, they can inspire their team to push through adversity and stay dedicated to their tasks.

Empathy, the ability to understand and share the feelings of others, is crucial in managing a team under stress. It involves listening actively, recognizing team members' emotions, and responding in a way that acknowledges their concerns. In a toxic environment, where misunderstandings and mistrust are rampant, empathy helps bridge gaps and build stronger connections. A project manager who practices empathy can better support their team, address grievances, and foster a sense of belonging and mutual respect.

Lastly, social skills encompass the ability to manage relationships and build networks. Effective communication, conflict resolution, and leadership are all part of this skill set. In a toxic work setting, strong social skills enable a project manager to navigate complex interpersonal dynamics, mediate disputes, and unite the team towards common goals. By fostering open communication and collaboration, they can counteract the divisive nature of the environment and cultivate a more cohesive and productive team.

Developing emotional intelligence is not an overnight process; it requires continuous effort and reflection. However, the benefits are manifold. A project manager equipped with emotional intelligence can transform a toxic environment, turning challenges into opportunities for growth and creating a resilient, motivated, and united team. This not only enhances the likelihood of project success but also contributes to a more positive and supportive workplace culture, where individuals feel valued and empowered to perform at their best.

Strengthening Team Cohesion

In the midst of a toxic environment, where negativity and discord can easily seep into the crevices of a project, there lies an imperative need to fortify the bonds among team members. The very fabric of a successful project often hinges on the strength of its team cohesion, a factor that can either make or break the overall outcome.

Creating a sense of unity among team members begins with establishing a shared vision. This vision serves as a beacon, guiding each individual towards a common goal. When every member understands the broader objective, their efforts become aligned, and the sense of belonging naturally follows. This alignment is not merely about tasks and deliverables but about instilling a sense of purpose that transcends the daily grind.

Communication stands as the cornerstone of team cohesion. Open, transparent, and frequent communication helps in building trust, a vital component in any team dynamic. In a toxic environment, where misunderstandings and miscommunications can run rampant, it becomes even more crucial to ensure that lines of communication remain clear and unobstructed. Regular team meetings, one-on-one check-ins, and informal gatherings can foster an atmosphere where team members feel heard and valued.

Another pivotal aspect is recognizing and valuing the individual strengths of each team member. In a toxic environment, it is easy for individuals to feel undervalued or overlooked. By acknowledging their unique contributions, a manager can boost morale and reinforce the notion that every role is essential to the project's success. This recognition can take various forms, from verbal appreciation during meetings to more formal acknowledgments like awards or incentives.

Conflict is inevitable in any team setting, but in a toxic environment, it can quickly escalate if not managed properly. It is essential to address conflicts head-on, with a focus on resolution rather than blame. Encouraging a culture of constructive feedback, where differences are discussed openly and respectfully, can prevent minor disagreements from snowballing into major rifts. Mediation and conflict resolution workshops can also equip team members with the tools they need to navigate interpersonal challenges effectively.

Fostering a sense of camaraderie through team-building activities can also play a significant role in strengthening team cohesion. These activities, whether they are simple ice-breakers or more elaborate retreats, provide opportunities for team members to connect on a personal level. Such connections can humanize colleagues, making it easier to empathize and collaborate with one another, even in the face of adversity.

Leadership plays a critical role in setting the tone for team cohesion. A leader who models positive behavior, demonstrates empathy, and remains approachable can inspire the same qualities in their team. Leading by example, a manager can create an environment where mutual respect and cooperation are the norms, rather than the exceptions.

Incorporating these strategies can transform a fragmented group of individuals into a cohesive unit, capable of weathering the storms of a toxic environment. By focusing on shared vision, open communication, individual recognition, conflict resolution, team-building, and strong leadership, a manager can cultivate a resilient and united team. This cohesion not only enhances the team's overall performance but also creates a more supportive and positive work environment, where each member feels empowered to contribute their best.

Developing Coping Mechanisms

Navigating through the treacherous waters of toxic project environments demands more than just technical prowess; it requires a robust set of coping mechanisms to maintain one's mental and emotional well-being. In the midst of ceaseless pressure, unyielding deadlines, and challenging interpersonal dynamics, the ability to develop and refine these mechanisms can make the difference between merely surviving and truly thriving.

In the heart of a toxic environment, stress can become an unwelcome constant companion. It is essential to recognize the early signs of stress and take proactive steps to mitigate its effects. Regular physical activity, even something as simple as a brisk walk, can work wonders. Exercise triggers the release of endorphins, the body's natural stress relievers, which can provide a much-needed boost in morale and energy.

Mindfulness practices are another powerful tool in the arsenal. Techniques such as meditation, deep-breathing exercises, and yoga can help center the mind, providing clarity and calm amidst chaos. These practices encourage a focus on the present moment, reducing the overwhelming feelings that often accompany toxic work settings. Allocating a few minutes each day to mindfulness can significantly enhance one's ability to handle stress and maintain a balanced perspective.

Establishing clear boundaries is crucial. In environments where work demands frequently spill over into personal time, it becomes vital to delineate where work ends and personal life begins. This might involve setting specific times for checking emails or turning off notifications after a certain hour. By creating these boundaries, one can protect personal time and prevent burnout.

Building a support network is another key strategy. Having a circle of trusted colleagues, friends, or mentors to confide in can provide emotional support and practical advice. These connections can offer a sense of solidarity and remind one that they are not alone in their struggles. Regularly scheduled check-ins with this support network can be a source of encouragement and a sounding board for ideas and frustrations alike.

Developing a problem-solving mindset can also be beneficial. Instead of viewing challenges as insurmountable obstacles, reframing them as opportunities for growth can shift one's perspective. This approach encourages a proactive stance, focusing on what can be controlled and improved rather than dwelling on the negative aspects of the environment.

Self-compassion is another essential element. In high-pressure settings, it is easy to fall into the trap of self-criticism. Acknowledging that it is okay to feel overwhelmed and giving oneself permission to take breaks can foster a healthier relationship with work. This approach emphasizes the importance of treating oneself with the same kindness and understanding that one would offer to a friend in a similar situation.

Lastly, seeking professional help should never be overlooked. Speaking with a therapist or counselor can provide additional strategies and insights tailored to one's specific circumstances. Professional guidance can be an invaluable resource for navigating the complexities of toxic environments, offering both support and practical tools for managing stress and maintaining mental health.

By integrating these coping mechanisms into daily routines, individuals can build resilience and maintain their well-being even in the most challenging project environments. These strategies not only contribute to personal health but also enhance overall productivity and job satisfaction, creating a more sustainable path forward in toxic work settings.

Encouraging Open Communication

In a project environment tainted by toxicity, fostering an atmosphere where team members feel comfortable expressing their thoughts and concerns is crucial. Open communication acts as the lifeline that binds the team together, enabling them to navigate through the murky waters of a challenging project landscape.

To set the stage for transparent dialogue, it is essential to establish a foundation of trust. Without trust, team members may hesitate to share their true thoughts, fearing backlash or negative consequences. Leaders must demonstrate reliability and integrity, consistently acting in the best interest of the team. This can be achieved by keeping promises, maintaining confidentiality, and showing genuine concern for the well-being of team members.

Creating regular opportunities for communication is another vital strategy. Scheduled meetings, both formal and informal, provide structured platforms for team members to voice their opinions. These gatherings should be designed to encourage participation from everyone, not just the most vocal members. Employing techniques such as round-robin discussions can ensure that each person has the chance to contribute.

Listening is a powerful tool in promoting open communication. Leaders and team members alike must practice active listening, which involves fully concentrating on the speaker, understanding their message, and responding thoughtfully. This practice not only validates the speaker's perspective but also fosters a deeper level of mutual respect and understanding. Leaders should model this behavior, setting a precedent for the rest of the team.

Feedback is another critical element in this dynamic. Constructive feedback helps team members grow and improve, but it must be delivered in a manner that is respectful and supportive. Feedback sessions should be framed as opportunities for development rather than criticism, focusing on behaviors and outcomes rather than personal attributes. Encouraging a culture where feedback is regularly exchanged and openly received can significantly enhance team cohesion and performance.

Transparency also plays a pivotal role in open communication. Team members should be kept informed about project developments, decisions, and changes. This openness reduces uncertainty and prevents the spread of misinformation, which can exacerbate the toxic environment. Leaders should strive to be as transparent as possible, sharing both the successes and the challenges faced by the project. This approach not only builds trust but also fosters a sense of shared responsibility and collective problem-solving.

Empathy is another cornerstone of effective communication in toxic environments. Understanding and acknowledging the emotions and perspectives of others can bridge gaps and resolve conflicts. Leaders should cultivate empathy by actively seeking to understand the experiences and feelings of their team members, and by showing compassion in their interactions.

Training and development can further bolster communication skills within the team. Workshops and seminars on effective communication, conflict resolution, and emotional intelligence can equip team members with the tools they need to navigate the complexities of a toxic environment. Investing in these areas demonstrates a commitment to improving the overall health and functionality of the team.

In addition, leveraging technology can facilitate open communication, especially in distributed or remote teams. Tools such as instant messaging, video conferencing, and collaborative platforms can bridge geographical gaps and ensure that communication flows seamlessly.

By prioritizing open communication, project leaders can transform a toxic environment into one where ideas are freely exchanged, concerns are promptly addressed, and the team operates with a sense of unity and purpose. This shift not only enhances project outcomes but also contributes to a more positive and productive work atmosphere.

Chapter 3: Effective Leadership Styles for Toxic Environments

Transformational Leadership

In the realm of project management, particularly within toxic environments, the role of leadership cannot be overstated. When navigating these fraught landscapes, a specific kind of leadership emerges as particularly effective—transformational leadership. This leadership style transcends traditional management approaches, aiming to inspire and elevate the entire team, fostering a sense of purpose and commitment that can overcome even the most challenging conditions.

Transformational leaders are characterized by their ability to influence and motivate their teams through a compelling vision. They possess an innate ability to articulate a clear and inspiring future, one that resonates deeply with the values and aspirations of their team members. This vision acts as a beacon, guiding the team through the murky waters of a toxic work environment, providing a sense of direction and hope.

At the core of transformational leadership is the concept of intellectual stimulation. Leaders who employ this approach encourage creativity and innovation, challenging their team members to think critically and solve problems in novel ways. This is particularly crucial in toxic environments, where traditional solutions may no longer be effective. By fostering an atmosphere of intellectual curiosity and open-mindedness, transformational leaders can help their teams to break free from the constraints of a negative work culture and develop innovative strategies to move forward.

Another key aspect of transformational leadership is individualized consideration. Leaders who practice this style take the time to understand the unique strengths, weaknesses, and aspirations of each team member. They offer personalized support and mentorship, helping individuals to grow and develop in their roles. This personal investment not only boosts morale but also builds a strong sense of loyalty and trust within the team. In toxic environments, where trust is often eroded, this individualized approach can be a powerful antidote, fostering a sense of community and mutual respect.

Transformational leaders also exhibit a high degree of emotional intelligence. They are adept at reading the emotional currents within their team and responding with empathy and understanding. This emotional attunement allows them to address conflicts and tensions proactively, creating a more harmonious and supportive work environment. In toxic settings, where emotions can run high and stress levels are elevated, this emotional intelligence is an invaluable asset, enabling leaders to navigate interpersonal dynamics with grace and sensitivity.

Moreover, transformational leaders lead by example. They embody the values and behaviors they wish to see in their team, setting a standard for excellence and integrity. Their actions are consistent with their words, creating a sense of authenticity and credibility. This alignment between words and actions is particularly important in toxic environments, where skepticism and distrust may be prevalent. By demonstrating consistency and reliability, transformational leaders can rebuild trust and establish a foundation of stability and respect.

In conclusion, transformational leadership offers a powerful framework for managing projects in toxic environments. By inspiring a shared vision, fostering intellectual stimulation, providing individualized consideration, demonstrating emotional intelligence, and leading by example, transformational leaders can create a positive and resilient team culture. This approach not only mitigates the negative impacts of a toxic environment but also empowers teams to achieve their full potential, driving success and innovation even in the most challenging circumstances.

Servant Leadership

Servant leadership represents a fundamental shift in the conventional paradigm of leadership, particularly in the context of managing projects in toxic environments. Unlike traditional leadership models that emphasize hierarchy, control, and authority, servant leadership focuses on the growth and well-being of team members and communities. This approach is especially crucial in toxic environments, where the morale and engagement of team members are often compromised.

Central to servant leadership is the leader's commitment to serve others. This means prioritizing the needs of the team over personal ambitions or organizational demands. By fostering an environment where team members feel valued and supported, a servant leader can mitigate the negative effects of a toxic workplace. This leadership style encourages open communication, empathy, and collaboration, which are essential for navigating the complexities and stressors of toxic environments.

A servant leader actively listens to their team, seeking to understand their concerns, aspirations, and ideas. This attentive approach helps in identifying the root causes of toxicity and addressing them effectively. By genuinely valuing the input of team members, a servant leader can create a culture of trust and mutual respect. This trust is the foundation upon which resilient and cohesive teams are built, capable of weathering the challenges posed by toxic environments.

Empathy is another cornerstone of servant leadership. In toxic environments, where stress and conflict are prevalent, empathetic leaders can provide the emotional support that team members need. By recognizing and acknowledging the struggles of their team, servant leaders can offer appropriate resources and solutions to alleviate stress and foster a more positive work environment. This empathetic approach not only enhances team morale but also improves overall productivity and job satisfaction.

Furthermore, servant leaders are committed to the personal and professional development of their team members. They invest time and resources in coaching, mentoring, and providing opportunities for growth. This developmental focus is particularly important in toxic environments, where employees may feel undervalued and stagnant. By empowering team members to develop their skills and advance their careers, servant leaders can inspire loyalty and dedication, which are vital for the success of any project.

Transparency and ethical behavior are also integral to servant leadership. In toxic environments, where distrust and unethical practices may be rampant, servant leaders stand out by consistently demonstrating integrity and honesty. They communicate openly about challenges and decisions, ensuring that team members are informed and involved. This transparency helps to dismantle the barriers of mistrust and fosters a culture of accountability and ethical conduct.

In practice, servant leadership requires a high level of self-awareness and a willingness to set aside personal ego. Leaders must be humble and ready to learn from their team, recognizing that leadership is not about exerting power but about enabling others to succeed. This humility is particularly important in toxic environments, where the misuse of power can exacerbate existing issues and hinder progress.

Implementing servant leadership in toxic environments can transform the workplace into a more inclusive, supportive, and productive space. By prioritizing the well-being of team members, fostering open communication, and committing to ethical behavior, servant leaders can effectively counteract the negative impacts of toxicity. This approach not only enhances the success of individual projects but also contributes to the long-term health and sustainability of the organization.

Situational Leadership

In environments where toxicity pervades, effective leadership becomes not just a requirement, but a lifeline. The essence of situational leadership lies in its adaptability, its fluidity in response to the ever-changing dynamics of project environments. At its core, this leadership style recognizes that one size does not fit all. Leaders must be chameleons, changing their approach based on the situation, the team's development level, and the specific challenges at hand.

Navigating through a toxic project environment demands acute awareness and keen judgment. Leaders must assess the maturity and competence of their team members, tailoring their guidance and support to fit individual needs. In some cases, directive leadership is paramount. When team members are inexperienced or demoralized, clear, authoritative directives can provide the structure and confidence needed to steer the project back on course. Conversely, when the team is seasoned and capable, a more delegative approach fosters autonomy and innovation, allowing team members to leverage their expertise without feeling micromanaged.

Communication is the cornerstone of situational leadership. In toxic environments, lines of communication are often frayed, trust is eroded, and misinformation can spread like wildfire. Leaders must prioritize open, honest, and consistent communication, ensuring that team members are well-informed and feel heard. It is not merely about disseminating information but also about listening actively, addressing concerns, and fostering a culture where feedback is valued and acted upon.

Empathy plays a critical role in this leadership style. Toxic environments can take a toll on morale and mental health. Leaders need to be attuned to the emotional and psychological states of their team members, providing support and understanding when needed. This might involve offering flexibility, recognizing and celebrating small victories, or simply being a compassionate ear. By acknowledging the human element within the team, leaders can mitigate some of the adverse effects of a toxic environment.

Situational leadership also demands a high degree of self-awareness. Leaders must constantly reflect on their own behaviors and attitudes, ensuring that they are not inadvertently contributing to the toxicity. This involves being receptive to feedback, recognizing personal biases, and being willing to adapt one's leadership style for the greater good of the project and the team.

In addition, situational leaders must be adept at conflict resolution. Toxic environments are often rife with interpersonal conflicts, power struggles, and political maneuvering. Leaders must possess the skills to navigate these turbulent waters, mediating disputes, and fostering a collaborative atmosphere. This requires patience, diplomacy, and the ability to remain impartial, focusing on the project's objectives rather than getting entangled in personal vendettas.

Flexibility is the hallmark of situational leadership. Leaders must be prepared to pivot strategies as the project evolves, responding to new challenges and opportunities with agility. This might involve shifting from a hands-on approach to a more hands-off one as the team gains confidence and proficiency. It also means being open to new ideas and approaches, encouraging creativity and innovation even in the face of adversity.

In toxic environments, the path to project success is fraught with obstacles. However, with situational leadership, leaders can navigate these challenges with finesse, adapting their approach to meet the needs of their team and the demands of the project. This dynamic, responsive leadership style not only helps to mitigate the effects of toxicity but also empowers teams to rise above the challenges, fostering resilience and driving project success.

Adaptive Leadership

Adaptive leadership is a dynamic and responsive approach crucial for navigating the complexities of toxic project environments. Unlike traditional leadership models that rely on established hierarchies and rigid protocols, adaptive leadership thrives on flexibility, emotional intelligence, and a keen understanding of the human elements involved in project management. This type of leadership is not just about making decisions; it's about understanding the underlying issues that drive behaviors and outcomes within a team.

In toxic environments, where stress and conflict are often prevalent, adaptive leaders must first recognize the signs of toxicity. These can manifest as low morale, high turnover rates, frequent conflicts, and a general sense of dissatisfaction among team members. Recognizing these signs early allows adaptive leaders to address the root causes rather than just the symptoms. They must be observant, empathetic, and skilled in reading both verbal and non-verbal cues.

Communication is a cornerstone of adaptive leadership. In toxic settings, open and honest communication can be a powerful antidote. Adaptive leaders foster an environment where team members feel safe to express their concerns and ideas without fear of retribution. This involves active listening, where leaders genuinely consider the input from their team and demonstrate that their voices are valued. By doing so, they can uncover hidden issues and work collaboratively to find solutions.

Another critical aspect of adaptive leadership is the ability to pivot and adjust strategies as circumstances change. In toxic environments, static plans are often rendered ineffective by unforeseen challenges and fluctuating team dynamics. Adaptive leaders are not afraid to change course when necessary. They are adept at assessing the situation, gathering relevant information, and making informed decisions that benefit the project and the team as a whole. This flexibility can be the difference between a project's success and failure in challenging environments.

Empathy plays a significant role in adaptive leadership. Understanding the personal and professional challenges faced by team members can help leaders provide the necessary support and resources. This might involve offering additional training, reallocating workloads, or simply providing a listening ear. By addressing individual needs, adaptive leaders can mitigate the effects of a toxic environment and foster a more positive and productive atmosphere.

Conflict resolution is another area where adaptive leadership shines. In toxic environments, conflicts are almost inevitable. Adaptive leaders do not shy away from these conflicts but rather approach them as opportunities for growth and improvement.

They facilitate discussions that aim to resolve issues constructively, ensuring that all parties feel heard and respected. This approach not only resolves immediate conflicts but also builds a foundation of trust and collaboration within the team.

Furthermore, adaptive leaders are committed to continuous learning and development, both for themselves and their team. They seek out new knowledge, skills, and perspectives that can help them better navigate the complexities of their environment. This commitment to growth ensures that they are always equipped to handle new challenges and can lead their team with confidence and competence.

In essence, adaptive leadership is about being attuned to the ever-changing dynamics of a toxic environment and responding with agility, empathy, and strategic foresight. It requires a deep understanding of human behavior, a commitment to open communication, and a willingness to continuously evolve. By embodying these principles, adaptive leaders can transform toxic environments into spaces where teams can thrive and succeed.

Chapter 4: Conflict Resolution Strategies

Understanding Conflict Sources

In the realm of project management, especially within toxic environments, understanding the root causes of conflict is pivotal. Conflicts in such environments are often more intricate and multifaceted, requiring a deeper comprehension of their origins to manage them effectively. Several sources can contribute to the emergence of conflict, each with its own set of complexities and nuances.

One primary source of conflict in toxic project environments is the clash of personalities. When individuals with differing temperaments, work ethics, and communication styles are compelled to collaborate, friction is almost inevitable. For instance, a highly detail-oriented team member may find it challenging to work with someone who takes a more high-level, big-picture approach. These personality differences can lead to misunderstandings and resentment, which, if not addressed, can escalate into significant conflicts.

Another significant source of conflict is the lack of clear roles and responsibilities. In many toxic environments, there is often ambiguity around who is accountable for what, leading to overlapping duties and missed tasks. This lack of clarity can create a breeding ground for blame and frustration. When team members are unsure of their roles, they may feel undervalued or overburdened, further exacerbating tensions within the group.

Communication breakdowns are also a prevalent source of conflict. In high-pressure projects, effective communication is crucial. However, in toxic environments, communication channels are often clogged with misinformation, assumptions, and a lack of transparency. Miscommunication can lead to misaligned expectations and erroneous conclusions, fostering an atmosphere of distrust and animosity. When team members do not feel heard or understood, their morale and cooperation can significantly deteriorate.

Resource constraints are another critical factor that can spark conflict. In many projects, particularly those operating under toxic conditions, there is a constant struggle for limited resources, be it time, money, or manpower. When resources are scarce, competition among team members can intensify, leading to conflicts over priorities and resource allocation. This competition can create a hostile work environment where collaboration is replaced by rivalry.

Differing priorities and goals among stakeholders can also be a major source of conflict. In any project, various stakeholders often have their own agendas and objectives. In a toxic environment, these differing priorities are magnified, leading to conflicts over the direction and focus of the project. When stakeholders are unable to align their goals, it can result in a fragmented approach, causing further discord and confusion.

Cultural differences within a team can also contribute to conflict. In today's globalized world, project teams are often composed of individuals from diverse cultural backgrounds. These differences can influence communication styles, decision-making processes, and conflict resolution approaches. If not managed properly, cultural misunderstandings can lead to significant conflicts, as team members may inadvertently offend or misinterpret each other's actions and intentions.

Understanding these sources of conflict is essential for any project manager operating in a toxic environment. By recognizing and addressing these root causes, it becomes possible to mitigate conflicts before they escalate, fostering a more collaborative and productive project atmosphere. Each source of conflict presents its own challenges, but with careful management and proactive measures, it is possible to navigate these complexities and steer the project towards success.

Mediation Techniques

Navigating the treacherous waters of toxic project environments requires more than just technical skills and experience; it demands a nuanced understanding of human behavior and the art of mediation. A project manager in such an environment must be adept at employing various mediation techniques to bring harmony and productivity to a fractured team. The first step in effective mediation is active listening. This involves more than just hearing the words spoken by team members; it requires understanding the underlying emotions and motivations. By genuinely listening, a project manager can identify the root causes of conflict and address them more effectively.

Another essential technique is neutrality. In a toxic environment, team members are often suspicious of one another and quick to assume bias. A project manager must remain impartial, avoiding any appearance of favoritism. This helps to build trust and encourages open communication. Neutrality also involves reframing the conversation to focus on common goals rather than personal grievances. When team members see that their concerns are being acknowledged without judgment, they are more likely to engage in constructive dialogue.

Facilitation is another critical mediation technique. It involves guiding discussions in a way that ensures everyone has a chance to speak and be heard. This can be particularly challenging in a toxic environment where voices of dissent are often silenced or ignored. A skilled facilitator can create a safe space for dialogue, encouraging quieter team members to share their perspectives and ensuring that dominant voices do not monopolize the conversation. Effective facilitation often requires setting ground rules for respectful communication and holding team members accountable for adhering to them.

The use of questioning techniques is also invaluable. Open-ended questions can help to uncover deeper issues and encourage team members to think critically about their positions. Questions like "What do you think is the main obstacle to our project's success?" or "How do you feel about the current team dynamics?" can provide insights that might not surface through direct confrontation. By asking thoughtful questions, a project manager can guide the team toward self-reflection and mutual understanding.

Conflict resolution skills are indispensable in toxic environments. This involves not only addressing conflicts as they arise but also anticipating potential flashpoints and defusing them before they escalate. Techniques such as conflict mapping can be useful for identifying the relationships and issues at the heart of disputes. By understanding the complexities of these relationships, a project manager can develop targeted strategies for resolution, whether through negotiation, compromise, or collaboration.

Empathy plays a vital role in mediation. Understanding the emotional states of team members and acknowledging their feelings can go a long way in de-escalating tensions. Empathy involves more than just sympathy; it requires a genuine effort to see the situation from another person's perspective. This can help to build rapport and foster a sense of unity within the team.

Lastly, follow-up is crucial. Mediation is not a one-time event but an ongoing process. After initial conflicts are addressed, a project manager must continue to monitor the team dynamics and provide support as needed. Regular check-ins and feedback sessions can help to maintain a positive atmosphere and prevent the re-emergence of toxic behaviors.

Incorporating these mediation techniques into daily project management practices can transform a toxic environment into a more collaborative and productive space. While the challenges are significant, the rewards of a harmonious and effective team are well worth the effort.

Negotiation Skills

In the intricate world of project management, especially within toxic environments, the ability to navigate negotiations becomes crucial. Projects are often plagued by conflicting interests, tight deadlines, and resource constraints. Each stakeholder has their own set of priorities, and aligning these can seem like an insurmountable challenge. The project manager must act as a mediator, finding common ground and fostering an atmosphere where collaboration can thrive despite the surrounding toxicity.

Understanding the context is the first step. Toxic environments are typically characterized by high levels of stress, mistrust, and a lack of clear communication. Recognizing these elements allows the project manager to approach negotiations with a mindset geared towards resolution rather than confrontation. It's about preparing mentally and emotionally to deal with potential resistance and conflict constructively.

Active listening is a foundational skill in this scenario. Often, stakeholders feel unheard or undervalued, which exacerbates the toxic atmosphere. By genuinely listening to their concerns, a project manager can uncover underlying issues that might not be immediately apparent. This not only demonstrates respect but also provides critical insights that can be used to craft solutions that address the root causes of dissatisfaction.

Empathy plays a significant role in negotiation within these challenging environments. Understanding the pressures and motivations of each stakeholder helps in framing discussions in a way that resonates with their needs. It's about seeing the project from their perspective and acknowledging their challenges. This empathetic approach can diffuse tensions and pave the way for more productive conversations.

Preparation cannot be overstated. Entering a negotiation without a clear plan is a recipe for failure. A project manager should have a thorough understanding of the project's goals, constraints, and the specific interests of each stakeholder. This includes anticipating objections and preparing counterarguments. The more informed and prepared the project manager is, the more confidently they can steer the negotiation towards a favorable outcome.

Flexibility and creativity are key. Toxic environments often require unconventional solutions. Being rigid in negotiations can lead to stalemates and further entrenchment of negative attitudes. Instead, a project manager should be open to exploring alternative approaches that might not have been considered initially. This willingness to adapt can unlock new pathways to agreement and progress.

The power of clear and transparent communication cannot be underestimated. Miscommunication is a common issue in toxic environments, often leading to misunderstandings and mistrust. By being clear about intentions, expectations, and constraints, a project manager can build a foundation of trust. Transparency helps in setting realistic expectations and reduces the likelihood of conflicts arising from unfulfilled promises or misaligned goals.

Building alliances is another strategic aspect. Identifying and cultivating relationships with key stakeholders who are open to collaboration can create a support network that eases the negotiation process. These allies can act as advocates for the project's goals and help sway others who may be more resistant.

Patience and persistence are virtues in these situations. Toxic environments are not transformed overnight, and negotiations can be drawn out and exhausting. Maintaining a calm and composed demeanor, even when faced with setbacks, is essential. The project manager must be willing to engage in ongoing dialogue and remain committed to finding a resolution, no matter how protracted the process may be.

In toxic environments, the stakes are high and the challenges numerous, but with the right negotiation skills, a project manager can turn potential conflicts into opportunities for collaboration and progress.

Building Consensus

Creating a harmonious environment in a toxic setting requires the delicate art of building consensus among team members. This process is pivotal to ensuring that everyone is aligned towards a common goal, despite the challenges posed by a negative atmosphere. The path to consensus is often fraught with obstacles, but with a strategic approach, it is possible to foster a collaborative spirit even in the most adverse conditions.

The first step in building consensus is to create an open forum for communication. In toxic environments, individuals often feel unheard or marginalized. Establishing a safe space where team members can express their opinions without fear of retribution is essential. This can be achieved through regular meetings, anonymous surveys, or suggestion boxes. The key is to ensure that everyone feels their voice is valued and that their input can make a difference.

Active listening plays a crucial role in this process. It is not enough to merely hear what team members are saying; one must also understand the underlying emotions and motivations behind their words. This requires patience and empathy. By acknowledging the concerns and suggestions of each individual, you demonstrate respect and foster a sense of belonging. This can significantly reduce the tension and animosity that often pervade toxic environments.

Transparent communication is another cornerstone of building consensus. Information should flow freely and openly among team members. When people are kept in the dark or fed half-truths, mistrust and suspicion can quickly grow. Clear, honest communication helps to build trust and ensures that everyone is on the same page. This includes sharing both the successes and the challenges faced by the team. Transparency fosters a culture of accountability and mutual respect.

It is also important to identify common goals and values. In toxic environments, individuals often focus on their differences rather than their shared objectives. By highlighting the common ground, you can create a sense of unity and purpose. This can be achieved through team-building exercises, workshops, or collaborative projects. When team members see that they are working towards a shared goal, they are more likely to put aside their differences and work together harmoniously.

Negotiation and compromise are integral to achieving consensus. In any group, there will be differing opinions and conflicting interests. The ability to negotiate and find a middle ground is essential. This requires a willingness to be flexible and to consider alternative perspectives. By facilitating constructive dialogue and encouraging compromise, you can help the team to arrive at mutually acceptable solutions.

Recognition and appreciation also play a vital role in building consensus. In a toxic environment, positive reinforcement is often lacking. Acknowledging the contributions and achievements of team members can boost morale and foster a sense of camaraderie. Simple gestures such as verbal praise, written commendations, or small rewards can go a long way in making individuals feel valued and appreciated.

Lastly, it is important to lead by example. As a leader, your behavior sets the tone for the rest of the team. Demonstrating integrity, fairness, and respect in your interactions can inspire others to follow suit. By embodying the principles of consensus-building, you can create a ripple effect that gradually transforms the toxic environment into a more positive and collaborative space.

Building consensus in a toxic environment is undoubtedly challenging, but with patience, empathy, and strategic communication, it is possible to foster a sense of unity and cooperation. Through open dialogue, transparency, common goals, negotiation, appreciation, and exemplary leadership, a toxic team can be guided towards a more harmonious and productive state.

Chapter 5: Maintaining Team Morale

Recognizing and Rewarding Effort

In the labyrinth of managing projects amidst toxic environments, one of the most critical yet often overlooked elements is the recognition and reward of effort. Amidst the chaos and challenges, where negativity can easily overshadow progress, acknowledging the dedication and hard work of team members becomes an essential tool for fostering a resilient and motivated workforce.

Imagine a project team working tirelessly against the backdrop of a hostile environment, where obstacles are not just external but also internal. Bureaucratic red tape, conflicting interests, and a pervasive sense of disillusionment can create a toxic atmosphere that saps the energy and morale of even the most dedicated professionals. In such a setting, the power of recognition cannot be understated. It serves as a beacon of hope, an affirmation that their efforts are not in vain.

Recognition in a toxic environment needs to be timely and sincere. A simple, heartfelt acknowledgment can work wonders. When a project manager takes the time to personally thank a team member for their hard work, it sends a powerful message. It tells the individual that their contributions are valued, that despite the surrounding negativity, their efforts are seen and appreciated. This can be done through verbal praise during meetings, personalized notes, or even public acknowledgment in front of peers. The key is to ensure that the recognition is specific and genuine.

Rewarding effort goes hand in hand with recognition but takes it a step further by offering tangible incentives. These rewards do not necessarily have to be grand or expensive. They can range from small tokens of appreciation, such as gift cards or an extra day off, to more significant rewards like bonuses or promotions. The aim is to make the team members feel that their hard work is not only noticed but also materially appreciated. This creates a positive reinforcement loop, motivating them to continue putting in their best efforts despite the challenges.

However, in toxic environments, it is crucial to ensure that the process of recognizing and rewarding effort is transparent and fair. Favoritism or perceived bias can exacerbate the toxicity, leading to resentment and further demoralization. Establishing clear criteria for rewards and ensuring that all team members have an equal opportunity to be recognized can help mitigate these risks. Regular reviews and feedback sessions can also provide a platform for discussing individual contributions and addressing any concerns about fairness.

Beyond individual recognition and rewards, fostering a culture of collective appreciation can also be beneficial. Celebrating team achievements, no matter how small, can help build camaraderie and a sense of shared purpose. Organizing team-building activities, acknowledging milestones, and creating opportunities for team members to express gratitude towards each other can strengthen the bonds within the team and create a more supportive environment.

In the face of adversity, the act of recognizing and rewarding effort becomes a powerful tool for project managers. It not only boosts morale and motivation but also helps in building a resilient and cohesive team capable of navigating the complexities of a toxic environment. By valuing and appreciating the hard work of their team members, project managers can create a more positive and productive atmosphere, even in the most challenging circumstances.

Promoting Work-Life Balance

In the midst of managing projects within toxic environments, the delicate equilibrium between professional responsibilities and personal well-being becomes paramount. Achieving such balance is not merely a matter of individual resilience but requires a concerted effort from both leaders and team members. Ensuring that employees do not feel perpetually tethered to their work is fundamental in fostering a healthy, productive environment.

Creating boundaries between work and personal time is essential. Encouraging employees to define clear start and end times for their workday can significantly reduce the risk of burnout. Leaders should model this behavior by respecting these boundaries themselves and refraining from sending work-related communications outside of designated hours. This practice not only demonstrates respect for personal time but also sets a precedent for the rest of the team.

Implementing flexible working arrangements can also play a crucial role. Flexibility allows employees to manage their time more effectively, accommodating personal commitments without compromising their professional responsibilities. This might include options such as remote work, flexible hours, or compressed workweeks. By providing such flexibility, organizations can help reduce stress and improve overall job satisfaction, even in the most demanding environments.

Support systems within the workplace are equally important. Establishing a culture where employees feel comfortable discussing their challenges and seeking support can make a significant difference. Regular check-ins and open-door policies can provide employees with the opportunity to voice their concerns and receive the necessary support. This can help to identify and address potential issues before they escalate, thereby maintaining a healthier work environment.

Offering resources for stress management and mental health support is another vital component. Workshops on stress reduction techniques, mindfulness practices, and access to counseling services can equip employees with the tools they need to manage stress effectively. Additionally, promoting physical health through initiatives like gym memberships, wellness programs, or even simple encouragement for regular breaks can contribute to overall well-being.

Recognition and appreciation of employees' efforts play a crucial role in maintaining morale. Regular acknowledgment of hard work and contributions can help to mitigate the negative effects of a toxic environment. This recognition can come in various forms, from verbal appreciation and written commendations to more tangible rewards. Feeling valued can significantly boost an employee's motivation and engagement, making it easier to navigate challenging work conditions.

Encouraging social connections within the team can also enhance work-life balance. Facilitating team-building activities and social events can help to foster a sense of community and support among colleagues. These connections can provide a vital support network, allowing employees to share experiences and offer mutual support, which can be particularly beneficial in high-stress environments.

Leaders must also be vigilant in identifying signs of imbalance or burnout among their team members. Being proactive in offering support and making necessary adjustments can prevent long-term negative consequences. This might involve redistributing workloads, providing additional resources, or even encouraging time off when needed.

By prioritizing these strategies, organizations can create a more balanced and supportive work environment. While the challenges of managing projects in toxic environments cannot be entirely eliminated, promoting work-life balance can significantly mitigate their impact. This holistic approach not only enhances employee well-being but also contributes to sustained productivity and overall organizational success.

Creating a Positive Work Culture

In the heart of every successful project lies a culture that nurtures positivity and collaboration. Establishing such an environment in toxic settings demands deliberate strategies and consistent effort. The essence of a positive work culture revolves around mutual respect, open communication, and a shared vision that aligns with both individual and organizational goals.

The foundation of a thriving work culture is built on trust. Trust is not merely given; it is earned through transparency and reliability. Leaders must demonstrate integrity and consistency in their actions. By doing so, they set a standard for the entire team. When team members trust their leaders and each other, they feel secure in voicing their opinions, sharing innovative ideas, and taking calculated risks without the fear of unwarranted criticism or retribution.

Communication is another critical pillar. In toxic environments, communication often breaks down, leading to misunderstandings and conflicts. To counteract this, fostering an atmosphere where open and honest dialogue is encouraged is vital. Regular team meetings, one-on-one check-ins, and an open-door policy can significantly enhance communication. Leaders should actively listen to their team members, validating their concerns and providing constructive feedback. This not only helps in addressing issues promptly but also makes individuals feel valued and heard.

Recognition and appreciation play a crucial role in cultivating positivity. Acknowledging the hard work and achievements of team members can boost morale and motivation. This can be achieved through formal recognition programs, as well as informal gestures like verbal praise or a simple thank-you note. Celebrating small victories and milestones can create a sense of accomplishment and camaraderie, reinforcing the collective effort towards common goals.

Empowerment is another key aspect. Providing team members with the autonomy to make decisions and take ownership of their tasks fosters a sense of responsibility and pride in their work. This can be facilitated by delegating meaningful tasks, offering opportunities for professional development, and encouraging creative problem-solving. When individuals feel empowered, they are more likely to be engaged and committed to the project's success.

Inclusive practices are essential in promoting a positive work culture. Embracing diversity and ensuring that every team member feels included and respected can lead to a more harmonious and productive environment. This involves being mindful of different perspectives and backgrounds, and actively working to eliminate biases and discrimination. Creating a culture of inclusion can enhance collaboration and innovation, as diverse teams bring a variety of ideas and solutions to the table.

Support and well-being cannot be overlooked. Providing resources for mental health and well-being, such as access to counseling services, wellness programs, and flexible work arrangements, can help team members manage stress and maintain a healthy work-life balance. Leaders should also model healthy behaviors, such as taking breaks and setting boundaries, to encourage their teams to do the same.

Building a positive work culture in a toxic environment is challenging, but not impossible. It requires a commitment to fostering trust, open communication, recognition, empowerment, inclusion, and well-being. By prioritizing these elements, leaders can transform a toxic environment into a thriving, collaborative, and productive space where projects can succeed and individuals can flourish.

Dealing with Burnout

Burnout is a silent predator in the realm of project management, especially within toxic environments. It creeps in slowly, often unnoticed until it has already taken a significant toll on one's mental and physical well-being. Recognizing and addressing burnout is crucial for maintaining not only personal health but also the overall success of the project.

The first signs of burnout are often subtle. A project manager might notice a persistent feeling of exhaustion, even after a full night's sleep. This fatigue is not just physical but also emotional, manifesting as a lack of enthusiasm for tasks that once brought satisfaction. Decision-making becomes increasingly challenging, and minor setbacks feel insurmountable. These symptoms, if ignored, can escalate into more severe health issues, including chronic stress, anxiety, and depression.

In toxic work environments, the risk of burnout is exacerbated by constant exposure to negativity, unrealistic demands, and a lack of support. The pressure to perform under such conditions can lead to a vicious cycle of overwork and diminishing returns. It is essential to break this cycle by implementing strategies to mitigate burnout.

Creating a supportive work culture is paramount. Encouraging open communication and fostering a sense of community can make a significant difference. Team members should feel safe to express their concerns without fear of retribution. Regular check-ins and feedback sessions can help identify early signs of burnout and address them promptly.

Time management is another critical aspect. It is important to set realistic goals and deadlines, allowing for adequate rest and recovery periods. Delegating tasks effectively can also alleviate some of the pressure. Trusting team members with responsibilities not only distributes the workload but also empowers them, fostering a more collaborative environment.

Self-care should not be overlooked. Encouraging team members to take breaks, engage in physical activity, and pursue hobbies outside of work can help maintain a healthy work-life balance. Mindfulness practices, such as meditation and deep-breathing exercises, can also be beneficial in managing stress levels.

Professional development opportunities can provide a sense of purpose and growth, counteracting the stagnation often felt in toxic environments. Investing in training and workshops can reinvigorate a team, equipping them with new skills and perspectives.

It is equally important to recognize and celebrate achievements, no matter how small. Acknowledging hard work and milestones can boost morale and provide a much-needed sense of accomplishment. This positive reinforcement can counterbalance the negativity inherent in toxic environments.

Seeking external support, such as counseling or coaching, can also be a valuable resource. Professional guidance can offer new coping strategies and provide an objective perspective on the challenges faced.

Ultimately, dealing with burnout requires a proactive and holistic approach. It involves not only addressing the symptoms but also tackling the root causes within the work environment. By fostering a culture of support, implementing effective time management strategies, and promoting self-care, project managers can navigate the challenges of toxic environments and safeguard both their well-being and the success of their projects.

Chapter 6: Communication Tactics for Toxic Environments

Active Listening Techniques

Within the tumultuous landscape of toxic work environments, the ability to listen actively stands as a beacon of hope and clarity. When navigating the treacherous waters of project management in such settings, the efficacy of communication often determines the success or failure of the endeavor. Active listening, an art often overshadowed by the urgency of tasks and the clamor of opinions, becomes an essential skill.

Imagine a scenario where team members are fraught with anxiety, mistrust, and frustration. Voices overlap, grievances are aired, yet solutions seem elusive. Here, the project manager must rise above the din, not by asserting dominance, but by truly hearing each individual. Active listening involves more than just hearing words; it requires an engagement of the mind and heart, an empathetic understanding of the underlying concerns and emotions.

One of the key techniques in active listening is mirroring. When a team member voices a concern, the project manager reflects back what has been said, both to confirm understanding and to show that the speaker's words hold value. For instance, if a team member expresses frustration about unrealistic deadlines, the manager might respond with, "I hear that you're feeling overwhelmed by the current deadlines and feel they are not achievable." This simple act of acknowledgment can diffuse tension and build a bridge of trust.

Another critical component is the use of open-ended questions. These questions encourage deeper dialogue and provide the speaker with an opportunity to explore their thoughts more fully. Instead of asking, "Are you okay with this task?" a manager might ask, "How do you feel about the current workload and the tasks assigned to you?" This invites a more comprehensive response and demonstrates genuine interest in the speaker's perspective.

Non-verbal cues also play a pivotal role in active listening. Eye contact, nodding, and appropriate facial expressions convey attentiveness and empathy. In a toxic environment, where suspicion and negativity may run high, these non-verbal signals can significantly enhance the communication process. They silently communicate respect and validate the speaker's feelings, fostering a sense of safety and openness.

Paraphrasing is another powerful technique. By rephrasing what the speaker has said in the listener's own words, the project manager can ensure clarity and prevent misunderstandings. For example, if a team member complains about the lack of resources, the manager might say, "So, you're saying that the current resources are insufficient for completing the project on time?" This not only confirms the manager's understanding but also gives the speaker a chance to correct any misinterpretations.

In the realm of toxic environments, emotions can run high and misunderstandings can be rampant. It's crucial for the project manager to maintain a calm and composed demeanor. This stability can be a soothing balm to an otherwise chaotic atmosphere. Techniques such as summarizing key points at the end of a discussion can also be beneficial. This ensures that everyone is on the same page and that important issues are not overlooked.

Active listening is not a passive act but a dynamic and interactive process. It requires patience, humility, and a genuine desire to understand others. In toxic environments, where communication breakdowns are common, mastering these techniques can transform the way teams interact and collaborate. By fostering a culture of listening, project managers can pave the way for more harmonious and productive work environments.

Non-Verbal Communication

Non-verbal communication plays an indispensable role in managing projects, particularly in toxic environments where tensions run high, and misunderstandings can escalate quickly. The subtle nuances of body language, facial expressions, and gestures can convey more than words ever could, providing critical insights into the true sentiments and intentions of team members.

In toxic environments, the stakes are higher, and non-verbal cues become even more significant. A project manager must develop a heightened sensitivity to these signals to navigate the complexities of interpersonal dynamics effectively. The way a person stands, the firmness of a handshake, or the direction of their gaze can reveal underlying issues that might not be expressed verbally. For instance, crossed arms and averted eyes during a meeting may indicate resistance or discomfort, signaling that there are unspoken concerns that need to be addressed.

Facial expressions are particularly telling in high-stress situations. A furrowed brow or a tight-lipped smile can speak volumes about a person's stress levels or dissatisfaction. Recognizing these signs early can provide an opportunity to address issues before they spiral out of control. The ability to read these cues accurately can also foster a sense of empathy and understanding, which is crucial for building trust and rapport in a strained environment.

Gestures and posture also contribute significantly to the communication landscape. Open gestures, such as a relaxed posture and open palms, can create an atmosphere of openness and honesty, encouraging team members to share their thoughts and concerns more freely. Conversely, closed gestures, such as clenched fists or hunched shoulders, can signal defensiveness or anxiety, suggesting that the individual might be feeling threatened or overwhelmed.

Eye contact, or the lack thereof, is another powerful form of non-verbal communication. Maintaining appropriate eye contact can convey confidence and sincerity, while avoiding eye contact can suggest evasiveness or discomfort. In a toxic environment, where trust may already be fragile, consistent and genuine eye contact can help to reinforce a sense of reliability and openness.

The tone and pace of voice, although technically a verbal element, also carry significant non-verbal weight. A calm and steady tone can help to de-escalate tension, while a rushed or high-pitched voice can exacerbate stress and anxiety. Paying attention to these vocal cues can provide additional context to the spoken words, helping to discern the true message being conveyed.

Proxemics, or the use of personal space, is another critical aspect of non-verbal communication. In a toxic environment, respecting personal boundaries becomes even more crucial. Encroaching on someone's personal space can be perceived as aggressive or intrusive, further heightening tensions. Conversely, maintaining an appropriate distance can convey respect and consideration, helping to ease interpersonal friction.

Understanding and effectively utilizing non-verbal communication can be a powerful tool for project managers working in toxic environments. By paying close attention to these subtle cues, a project manager can gain deeper insights into team dynamics, preempt potential conflicts, and foster a more collaborative and supportive atmosphere. The ability to read and respond to non-verbal signals can make the difference between a project that flounders in a toxic environment and one that thrives despite the challenges.

Assertiveness without Aggression

Navigating the turbulent waters of toxic project environments demands a delicate balance of firmness and tact. Project managers often find themselves walking a tightrope, needing to assert their authority and maintain control without tipping into the realm of aggression. This balance is crucial for fostering a productive atmosphere, especially when dealing with difficult stakeholders or team members who may be contributing to the toxicity.

Imagine a project meeting where tensions are running high. Deadlines are looming, resources are stretched thin, and the blame game is in full swing. In such a scenario, the project manager must step in decisively to steer the conversation towards constructive solutions. Assertiveness here means clearly stating expectations, setting boundaries, and holding individuals accountable—all while maintaining a calm and composed demeanor. It's about expressing needs and concerns confidently without resorting to hostility or intimidation.

Effective communication lies at the heart of assertiveness. When addressing issues, it's essential to focus on specific behaviors and their impact on the project, rather than making personal attacks. For instance, instead of saying, "You always miss deadlines," a more assertive approach would be, "The missed deadlines have delayed our project timeline. How can we ensure we meet future deadlines?" This method not only highlights the problem but also opens the door for collaborative problem-solving.

Body language and tone of voice play significant roles in how messages are perceived. Standing tall, making eye contact, and speaking in a steady, clear voice can convey confidence and authority without appearing aggressive. Conversely, crossed arms, a raised voice, or a confrontational stance can escalate tensions and detract from the message being conveyed.

In toxic environments, it's also important to recognize and manage one's emotional responses. Stress and frustration are natural reactions to challenging situations, but allowing these emotions to dictate behavior can lead to aggressive outbursts. Practicing emotional intelligence—being aware of one's emotions and managing them effectively—can help maintain composure and respond assertively rather than reactively.

Setting boundaries is another crucial aspect of assertiveness. In a toxic environment, there may be individuals who attempt to undermine authority or push back against decisions. Establishing clear boundaries about acceptable behavior and communication can prevent such actions from derailing the project. For example, if a team member consistently interrupts or disregards meeting protocols, addressing this behavior directly and outlining the expected conduct can reinforce the manager's authority and promote a more respectful atmosphere.

It's also beneficial to develop a repertoire of assertive techniques tailored to different scenarios. Techniques such as the broken record, where the manager calmly and repeatedly states their position, can be effective in situations where someone is persistently challenging authority. Another technique, fogging, involves acknowledging the other person's concerns while maintaining one's position, which can diffuse confrontations and foster mutual respect.

Practicing assertiveness without aggression not only helps in managing toxic environments but also sets a positive example for the team. It encourages open communication, mutual respect, and a collaborative spirit, which are essential for the successful completion of any project. Balancing assertiveness with empathy and understanding can transform a toxic environment into one where challenges are met with resilience and teamwork.

Managing Upward Communication

Effective upward communication in toxic project environments is a nuanced art that requires a blend of strategy, empathy, and tact. Project managers must navigate a labyrinth of organizational politics, power dynamics, and often, entrenched negative attitudes. The goal is to convey critical project information to senior management while mitigating potential backlash or misinterpretation.

A primary step is understanding the communication preferences and priorities of the senior management team. Each leader may have a unique style of receiving and processing information. Some may prefer detailed reports, while others might favor concise summaries or visual presentations. Tailoring communication to align with these preferences can significantly enhance receptivity and understanding.

Building a foundation of trust is critical. Trust can be established by consistently providing accurate, timely, and relevant information. This involves not only sharing successes but also being transparent about challenges and setbacks. In toxic environments, there may be a tendency to hide or downplay problems to avoid negative repercussions. However, honest communication fosters credibility and can lead to more constructive problem-solving discussions.

Navigating the power dynamics within the organization involves recognizing the influence and interests of various stakeholders. Identifying key allies and understanding their motivations can help in framing messages that resonate and garner support. It is also important to be aware of potential adversaries and anticipate their objections or concerns. Crafting messages that preemptively address these can reduce resistance and foster a more collaborative atmosphere.

Empathy plays a crucial role in managing upward communication. Understanding the pressures and constraints faced by senior management can inform the way messages are framed. Acknowledging their challenges and presenting information in a way that aligns with their priorities can make them more receptive to the communication. This might involve highlighting how project outcomes align with broader organizational goals or addressing potential risks in a manner that demonstrates proactive management.

Strategic timing is another important consideration. Choosing the right moment to communicate can significantly impact the reception of the message. This might involve waiting for a less stressful period or capitalizing on a positive development within the project or organization. Timing messages to coincide with key decision-making points can also enhance their influence.

Framing messages constructively is essential. In toxic environments, negative framing can exacerbate existing tensions and lead to defensive reactions. Instead, presenting challenges as opportunities for improvement or highlighting potential solutions can foster a more positive and collaborative dialogue. This involves careful wording and a focus on actionable insights rather than merely pointing out problems.

Regular, structured communication channels can also aid in managing upward communication. Establishing routine updates, whether through formal reports, meetings, or dashboards, creates a predictable and consistent flow of information. This not only keeps senior management informed but also reduces the likelihood of surprises, which can be particularly destabilizing in toxic environments.

Feedback mechanisms are equally important. Encouraging and actively seeking feedback from senior management can provide valuable insights into their perspectives and concerns. This can inform future communications and help in refining strategies to better align with their expectations and needs.

In essence, managing upward communication in toxic project environments requires a delicate balance of strategy, empathy, and tactical acumen. By understanding senior management's preferences, building trust, navigating power dynamics, empathizing with their challenges, timing communications effectively, framing messages constructively, establishing regular channels, and seeking feedback, project managers can enhance the effectiveness of their upward communication and foster a more supportive environment for project success.

Chapter 7: Risk Management in Adverse Conditions

Identifying Potential Risks

Navigating the treacherous waters of project management in toxic environments demands a keen eye for potential risks. In such challenging settings, the landscape is fraught with numerous hazards that can derail progress and undermine success. The first step in managing these projects effectively is to identify and understand the myriad of risks that can arise.

Toxic environments are characterized by negative elements such as poor communication, lack of trust, high stress levels, and adversarial relationships. These elements can introduce a plethora of risks that are not typically encountered in more neutral or positive settings. To begin with, one must consider the human factor. Team members in toxic environments often operate under significant stress and pressure, which can lead to burnout, decreased productivity, and increased turnover. The emotional and psychological toll on individuals can manifest in various ways, from absenteeism to outright conflict, each posing a threat to the project's success.

Communication breakdowns are another critical risk in toxic environments. When open and honest communication is stifled, misunderstandings and misinformation can proliferate. This can result in misaligned objectives, duplicated efforts, and missed deadlines. Effective communication is the bedrock of any successful project, and its absence can be particularly detrimental when navigating the complexities of a toxic environment.

Furthermore, trust, or the lack thereof, plays a significant role in the dynamics of a project. In toxic settings, trust is often in short supply, leading to a culture of suspicion and blame. This can hinder collaboration and cooperation among team members, as individuals may be more inclined to protect their own interests rather than working towards the common goal. The erosion of trust can also extend to stakeholders, who may become wary and less supportive, further complicating project execution.

The organizational culture in toxic environments can also pose substantial risks. A culture that promotes negativity, competition over collaboration, and punitive measures can stifle innovation and creativity. Team members may be less willing to take risks or propose new ideas, fearing retribution or criticism. This can lead to stagnation and a lack of progress, as the project becomes mired in a cycle of fear and inaction.

Another significant risk to consider is the potential for resource constraints. In toxic environments, resources such as time, money, and personnel are often mismanaged or allocated inefficiently. This can stem from poor leadership, lack of clear direction, or internal power struggles. The resulting resource shortages can severely impact the project's timeline and deliverables, forcing the team to make difficult trade-offs that could compromise quality and scope.

Finally, external factors must not be overlooked. Toxic environments often create a ripple effect that extends beyond the immediate team or organization. Negative reputations can precede the project, affecting relationships with external partners, vendors, and clients. This can lead to increased scrutiny, reduced cooperation, and even the withdrawal of critical support, all of which can jeopardize the project's viability.

In summary, identifying potential risks in toxic environments requires a comprehensive and nuanced approach. It is essential to consider the human, communicative, cultural, and resource-related factors that can influence project outcomes. By thoroughly understanding these risks, project managers can develop strategies to mitigate their impact and navigate the complexities of toxic environments more effectively.

Developing Risk Mitigation Plans

Risk mitigation is a critical component in managing projects within toxic environments. Understanding that such environments are fraught with uncertainties and potential hazards, developing comprehensive risk mitigation plans becomes indispensable. The first step in this intricate process involves identifying the risks that could jeopardize the project's success. This requires a thorough examination of both internal and external factors. Internal factors may include team dynamics, resource availability, and organizational culture, while external factors could encompass market volatility, regulatory changes, and environmental conditions.

Once risks are identified, the next phase involves a detailed analysis to assess their potential impact and likelihood. This is often achieved through qualitative and quantitative methods. Qualitative analysis might involve expert judgment, historical data review, and scenario analysis, while quantitative analysis could incorporate statistical models, probability distributions, and sensitivity analysis. The goal is to prioritize risks based on their potential to disrupt the project. High-priority risks demand immediate attention and robust mitigation strategies, whereas lower-priority risks might be monitored with less intensive measures.

Developing risk mitigation plans requires a collaborative approach. Engaging stakeholders, including project team members, sponsors, and external experts, ensures that diverse perspectives are considered. This collective input aids in crafting more comprehensive and effective mitigation strategies. It is also essential to foster an environment of open communication, where team members feel empowered to voice concerns and suggest solutions. Transparent communication not only enhances the quality of the risk mitigation plan but also builds trust and accountability within the team.

A well-constructed risk mitigation plan outlines specific actions to address identified risks. These actions may include risk avoidance, where certain activities are altered or eliminated to sidestep the risk entirely; risk reduction, where measures are taken to lessen the impact or likelihood of the risk; risk transfer, where the risk is shifted to a third party, such as through insurance or outsourcing; and risk acceptance, where the risk is acknowledged, and contingency plans are put in place to manage its consequences. Each mitigation strategy must be tailored to the unique context of the project and the nature of the risks involved.

Implementing the mitigation plan is a dynamic process that requires ongoing monitoring and adjustment. This involves regular risk reviews, progress assessments, and updates to the mitigation strategies as new information becomes available or as the project evolves. Effective monitoring tools and techniques, such as risk registers, dashboards, and key performance indicators, play a crucial role in tracking the effectiveness of the mitigation efforts. It is also important to document lessons learned and best practices, which can inform future projects and enhance organizational resilience.

In toxic environments, where the stakes are high, and the margin for error is slim, a proactive approach to risk mitigation is essential. By systematically identifying, analyzing, and addressing risks, project managers can navigate the complexities and uncertainties inherent in such settings. This not only safeguards the project's objectives but also contributes to a culture of risk awareness and continuous improvement.

Implementing Risk Response Strategies

Navigating through the complexities of managing projects in toxic environments often necessitates a robust approach to addressing risks. The identification and analysis of these potential pitfalls are only the beginning. The real challenge lies in devising and executing risk response strategies that can effectively mitigate the impact of adverse conditions and steer the project towards success.

The first step in implementing risk response strategies is to clearly define the specific actions that need to be taken. This involves a thorough understanding of the nature of each identified risk and the potential consequences it may have on the project. It is crucial to prioritize risks based on their severity and likelihood. High-priority risks require immediate attention and may necessitate more comprehensive response plans, while lower-priority risks can be monitored and addressed as needed.

Developing a risk response plan involves selecting the appropriate strategy for each risk. Common strategies include avoidance, mitigation, transfer, and acceptance. Avoidance entails altering the project plan to eliminate the risk entirely, which might involve changing project scope or objectives. Mitigation focuses on reducing the probability or impact of the risk through proactive measures. Transfer shifts the risk to a third party, such as through insurance or outsourcing certain project components. Acceptance involves acknowledging the risk and preparing to manage its consequences without attempting to alter its likelihood or impact.

Once the strategies are selected, it is essential to assign clear responsibilities and timelines for their implementation. This ensures that all team members are aware of their roles in managing risks and that there is accountability for executing the response plans. Regular communication and updates on the status of risk response activities are vital to maintain transparency and ensure that everyone is aligned with the overall risk management objectives.

Effective risk response also requires continuous monitoring and reassessment. The dynamic nature of toxic environments means that new risks can emerge, and existing risks can evolve. Regular risk reviews and updates to the risk response plan are necessary to address these changes. This might involve revisiting the initial risk assessment, adjusting response strategies, and reallocating resources as needed.

Documentation plays a critical role in the implementation of risk response strategies. Detailed records of risk assessments, response plans, and actions taken provide a valuable reference for future projects and help in the continuous improvement of risk management practices. It also ensures that there is a clear trail of accountability and that lessons learned can be captured and applied.

Engaging stakeholders throughout the process is another key element. Their input and support can provide valuable insights and resources for managing risks. Open and honest communication with stakeholders about the risks and the measures being taken to address them helps build trust and ensures that there is a shared understanding of the project's risk landscape.

Ultimately, the success of risk response strategies in toxic environments hinges on a proactive and disciplined approach. It requires a commitment to ongoing assessment, adaptability in response plans, and the active involvement of the entire project team. By systematically addressing risks and implementing well-defined response strategies, project managers can navigate the challenges of toxic environments and drive their projects towards successful outcomes.

Monitoring and Controlling Risks

In the intricate landscape of managing projects within toxic environments, the task of monitoring and controlling risks assumes a critical significance. The volatile nature of such environments necessitates a vigilant and proactive approach to ensure the project's stability and success. The process begins with establishing a robust risk management framework, tailored specifically to the unique challenges posed by toxic settings.

A cornerstone of this framework is the continuous identification and assessment of risks. This involves not only recognizing potential hazards but also understanding their implications on the project's objectives. The dynamic nature of toxic environments means that risks can evolve rapidly, requiring project managers to maintain an agile and responsive mindset. Regular risk assessments, therefore, become indispensable. These assessments should be scheduled at frequent intervals and supplemented by ad-hoc evaluations whenever significant changes occur in the project environment.

To facilitate effective risk monitoring, the deployment of advanced tools and technologies is essential. Risk management software, for instance, can provide real-time data analytics, enabling project managers to track risk indicators and trends. These tools can integrate with other project management systems, offering a holistic view of the project's health and highlighting areas that require immediate attention. The use of such technologies not only enhances the accuracy of risk monitoring but also accelerates the decision-making process, allowing for swift and informed responses.

Communication plays a pivotal role in the risk management process. Establishing clear and open channels of communication among all stakeholders ensures that risk-related information is disseminated promptly and accurately. Regular risk review meetings, involving project team members, sponsors, and other key stakeholders, provide a platform for discussing emerging risks and devising appropriate mitigation strategies. These meetings should be structured to encourage transparency and collaboration, fostering a collective responsibility towards managing risks.

The implementation of risk response strategies is the next critical step. These strategies should be diverse and flexible, capable of addressing a wide range of scenarios. Preventive measures, aimed at reducing the likelihood of risks occurring, are fundamental. These include stringent safety protocols, regular training sessions for team members, and the establishment of contingency plans. On the other hand, corrective measures, designed to mitigate the impact of risks that have materialized, are equally important. This could involve reallocating resources, adjusting project timelines, or revising project scopes to accommodate unforeseen challenges.

An often-overlooked aspect of risk management in toxic environments is the psychological well-being of the project team. The constant pressure of navigating risks can take a toll on team members, affecting their performance and decision-making abilities. Providing support mechanisms, such as counseling services and stress management programs, can help in maintaining a resilient and motivated team. Acknowledging and addressing the human element in risk management is crucial for sustaining long-term project success.

Documentation is another vital component of risk management. Keeping detailed records of identified risks, assessment results, and implemented responses ensures that there is a comprehensive repository of knowledge to refer to. This documentation not only aids in tracking the effectiveness of risk management efforts but also serves as a valuable resource for future projects. Learning from past experiences enables project managers to refine their risk management practices continually.

In the realm of toxic environments, the ability to monitor and control risks effectively can make the difference between project success and failure. It demands a meticulous and adaptive approach, underpinned by robust frameworks, advanced tools, and a collaborative mindset. By fostering an environment of vigilance and preparedness, project managers can navigate the complexities of toxic settings, safeguarding their projects against the myriad of challenges they may encounter.

Chapter 8: Enhancing Productivity Despite Challenges

Streamlining Processes

In environments where toxicity seeps into every corner, managing projects can feel like navigating a minefield. The key to not only surviving but thriving in such conditions lies in the ability to streamline processes. This involves a meticulous approach to refining workflows, eliminating redundancies, and ensuring that every step taken is purposeful and efficient.

The first step in this transformation is to conduct a thorough assessment of the existing processes. This means diving deep into current workflows, understanding the intricacies of each task, and identifying bottlenecks that hinder progress. Often, toxicity in a workplace can lead to convoluted procedures, either as a result of overcompensation for past mistakes or due to a lack of clear direction. By mapping out each process in detail, it becomes possible to see where inefficiencies lie and where improvements can be made.

Once the assessment is complete, the focus shifts to simplification. Simplifying processes involves stripping away unnecessary steps and focusing on the core actions that drive the project forward. This can be achieved by leveraging modern project management tools that provide clear visual representations of workflows. These tools can highlight dependencies, critical paths, and potential delays, allowing for a more streamlined approach to task management.

Communication is another critical element in streamlining processes. In toxic environments, communication often suffers, leading to misunderstandings, duplicated efforts, and missed deadlines. Establishing clear, consistent channels of communication can mitigate these issues. Regular meetings, transparent reporting, and the use of collaborative platforms ensure that everyone is on the same page and that information flows smoothly across the team.

Standardization plays a pivotal role in refining processes. By developing standardized procedures for common tasks, teams can reduce variability and ensure that everyone follows the same protocols. This not only enhances efficiency but also fosters a sense of predictability and stability, which is crucial in a toxic environment. Standard operating procedures (SOPs), checklists, and templates can be invaluable tools in achieving this standardization.

Another aspect to consider is the delegation of tasks. In a toxic environment, there can be a tendency for micromanagement, which stifles creativity and slows down progress. Empowering team members by delegating tasks according to their strengths and expertise can lead to more efficient workflows. Trusting the team to take ownership of their responsibilities can improve morale and productivity, creating a more positive working atmosphere.

Continuous improvement is a philosophy that must be ingrained in the team's culture. This means regularly reviewing processes, soliciting feedback, and making adjustments as needed. In a toxic environment, complacency can be particularly detrimental. By fostering a mindset of constant evaluation and refinement, teams can adapt to changing circumstances and continuously enhance their efficiency.

Technology can also be a powerful ally in streamlining processes. Automation tools can handle repetitive tasks, freeing up team members to focus on more complex and strategic activities. Project management software can provide real-time insights into progress, resource allocation, and potential risks, enabling more informed decision-making.

Ultimately, the goal of streamlining processes in a toxic environment is to create a more efficient, cohesive, and resilient team. By assessing and simplifying workflows, enhancing communication, standardizing procedures, delegating effectively, embracing continuous improvement, and leveraging technology, project managers can navigate the challenges of a toxic workplace and steer their projects toward success.

Prioritizing Tasks Effectively

In the midst of managing projects within toxic environments, where stress levels run high and resources are often scarce, the ability to prioritize tasks effectively becomes a lifeline. The chaos and unpredictability that characterize toxic environments make it imperative to distinguish between what is urgent and what is important. This distinction is crucial for ensuring that efforts are directed towards tasks that truly matter, rather than being swallowed by the clamor of immediate but inconsequential demands.

Task prioritization begins with a clear understanding of project goals and objectives. When the overarching aims are well-defined, it becomes easier to align daily tasks with these larger aspirations. This alignment ensures that every action taken contributes to the forward momentum of the project, rather than diverting energy into unproductive avenues. In toxic environments, where distractions are plentiful and pressures are intense, a clearly articulated vision serves as an anchor, providing direction and focus.

One effective method for prioritizing tasks is the Eisenhower Matrix, which categorizes tasks based on their urgency and importance. By plotting tasks into four quadrants—urgent and important, important but not urgent, urgent but not important, and neither urgent nor important—project managers can visualize where their attention is most needed. Tasks that fall into the "urgent and important" category should be addressed immediately, as they are critical to both the project's success and its timely completion. Conversely, tasks that are neither urgent nor important can be delegated or postponed, freeing up valuable time and resources for more pressing matters.

In toxic environments, the ability to delegate effectively becomes even more vital. Delegation not only helps in managing workload but also empowers team members, fostering a sense of ownership and accountability. However, delegation must be approached with care. It's essential to match tasks with the right individuals, considering their skills, experience, and current workload. Clear communication of expectations and deadlines ensures that tasks are executed efficiently and to the required standard.

Another important aspect of prioritizing tasks is flexibility. Toxic environments are often marked by constant change and unforeseen challenges. A rigid approach to task management can lead to frustration and inefficiency. Instead, adopting a dynamic prioritization strategy allows project managers to respond swiftly to new information and shifting circumstances. Regularly reviewing and adjusting priorities ensures that the project remains on track, even when faced with unexpected obstacles.

Effective communication is a cornerstone of successful task prioritization. In environments where misunderstandings and miscommunications can easily exacerbate tensions, maintaining clear and open lines of communication is essential. Regular team meetings, progress updates, and feedback sessions help ensure that everyone is aligned and aware of current priorities. This shared understanding minimizes the risk of duplicated efforts and ensures that the team can respond cohesively to any changes in direction.

Time management tools and techniques can also play a significant role in prioritizing tasks. Tools like Gantt charts, Kanban boards, and project management software provide visual representations of task timelines and dependencies, aiding in the identification of critical path activities. These tools help in planning and scheduling tasks more effectively, ensuring that deadlines are met and resources are utilized efficiently.

In essence, prioritizing tasks effectively in toxic environments requires a combination of strategic planning, flexible adaptation, and clear communication. By focusing on what truly matters and maintaining a dynamic approach to task management, project managers can navigate the complexities of toxic environments and steer their projects towards successful outcomes.

Utilizing Technology for Efficiency

In the realm of project management, especially within toxic environments, the strategic use of technology is indispensable for achieving efficiency and maintaining control over complex variables. The integration of advanced tools and platforms allows project managers to streamline processes, enhance communication, and ensure that every aspect of the project is meticulously monitored and adjusted as needed.

Modern project management software offers a plethora of features designed to tackle the unique challenges posed by toxic environments. These tools facilitate real-time collaboration, enabling team members to share updates, documents, and feedback instantaneously. This level of connectivity is crucial in environments where miscommunication can lead to significant setbacks or exacerbate existing tensions. With centralized dashboards, project managers can oversee the progress of various tasks, identify bottlenecks, and reallocate resources swiftly to maintain momentum.

Automation plays a pivotal role in reducing the manual workload and minimizing human error. By automating routine tasks such as scheduling, reporting, and tracking, project managers can focus their attention on more strategic aspects of the project. Automated alerts and notifications ensure that deadlines are met, and any deviations from the plan are promptly addressed. This proactive approach helps in mitigating risks and maintaining a steady course even in the face of adversity.

Data analytics and reporting tools are invaluable in toxic environments where decision-making must be informed by accurate and up-to-date information. These tools provide insights into performance metrics, resource utilization, and potential risks. By analyzing historical data, project managers can identify patterns and trends that may impact the project's success. Predictive analytics can forecast potential issues before they arise, allowing for preemptive measures to be put in place. This level of foresight is crucial for navigating the complexities and uncertainties inherent in toxic environments.

Communication platforms integrated with project management tools ensure that all stakeholders are kept in the loop. Whether it's through instant messaging, video conferencing, or collaborative document editing, these platforms break down silos and foster a culture of transparency and inclusiveness.

Regular check-ins and updates ensure that everyone is aligned with the project goals and aware of their responsibilities. This cohesive approach helps in building trust and reducing the friction that often plagues toxic environments.

Risk management tools are essential for identifying, assessing, and mitigating potential threats to the project. These tools enable project managers to create risk matrices, prioritize risks based on their impact and likelihood, and develop contingency plans. By systematically addressing risks, project managers can prevent minor issues from escalating into major crises. This structured approach to risk management is vital for maintaining stability and resilience in challenging environments.

Resource management tools help in optimizing the allocation and utilization of resources. In toxic environments, where resources may be scarce or under constant threat, efficient resource management is critical. These tools provide visibility into resource availability, skill sets, and workload distribution. By ensuring that resources are deployed effectively, project managers can avoid burnout, enhance productivity, and achieve project milestones within the stipulated timelines.

The use of technology extends to stakeholder management as well. Tools that facilitate stakeholder analysis, engagement, and feedback collection are crucial for managing expectations and fostering positive relationships. In toxic environments, where stakeholder dynamics can be particularly volatile, these tools help in maintaining a balanced and constructive dialogue.

Incorporating technology into project management not only enhances efficiency but also empowers project managers to navigate the complexities of toxic environments with confidence and precision. By leveraging the right tools and platforms, project managers can transform challenges into opportunities for growth and success.

Eliminating Productivity Blockers

Navigating the treacherous waters of toxic work environments requires more than just a sturdy ship; it demands a keen eye for identifying and eliminating the hidden reefs that can impede progress. Productivity blockers, those insidious obstacles that lurk beneath the surface, often go unnoticed until they have already caused significant damage. They come in various forms, from inefficient processes and unclear objectives to interpersonal conflicts and a lack of resources. Addressing these blockers is crucial for steering the project towards success.

One of the most pervasive productivity blockers is poor communication. In toxic environments, communication breakdowns are common, often resulting from a culture of mistrust or a lack of transparency. Misunderstandings and misinformation can quickly derail a project. To counteract this, establishing clear channels of communication is essential. Regular updates, open forums for discussion, and a culture that encourages honest feedback can help mitigate the risks associated with poor communication. Tools like project management software can also aid in keeping everyone on the same page.

Another significant blocker is unclear roles and responsibilities. When team members are unsure of their duties, tasks can either be duplicated or neglected entirely. This confusion can be exacerbated by the toxic environment, where fear and uncertainty may prevent individuals from seeking clarity. Defining roles and responsibilities at the outset of the project and revisiting them regularly can help ensure that everyone knows what is expected of them. Visual aids like RACI charts, which outline who is Responsible, Accountable, Consulted, and Informed for each task, can be particularly useful.

Interpersonal conflicts are another common productivity blocker in toxic environments. These conflicts can arise from personality clashes, competition for resources, or differing work styles. Left unaddressed, they can create a hostile work environment that stifles creativity and collaboration. Mediating conflicts promptly and fairly is crucial. Encouraging a culture of respect and understanding, where differences are viewed as strengths rather than weaknesses, can help foster a more harmonious work environment. Team-building activities and conflict resolution training can also be beneficial.

Resource constraints, whether in terms of time, money, or materials, can severely hamper productivity. In a toxic environment, these constraints are often exacerbated by poor planning and mismanagement. Conducting a thorough resource assessment at the beginning of the project can help identify potential shortfalls. Regularly reviewing resource allocation and making adjustments as necessary can also help ensure that the project stays on track. Leveraging external resources, such as consultants or temporary staff, can provide additional support when internal resources are stretched thin.

Lastly, a lack of motivation and morale can be a significant productivity blocker. In toxic environments, employees may feel undervalued, overworked, or disconnected from the project's goals. This can lead to disengagement and a decrease in overall productivity. Recognizing and rewarding hard work, providing opportunities for professional growth, and fostering a sense of purpose can help boost morale. Regular check-ins with team members to gauge their well-being and address any concerns can also contribute to a more motivated and productive workforce.

Eliminating productivity blockers in a toxic environment is a multifaceted challenge that requires vigilance, empathy, and strategic planning. By identifying and addressing the root causes of these blockers, project managers can create a more conducive environment for success. The journey may be fraught with difficulties, but the rewards of a cohesive, efficient, and motivated team are well worth the effort.

Chapter 9: Leveraging Diversity in Toxic Environments

Understanding Diverse Perspectives

In the realm of project management, especially within environments that can be considered toxic, understanding the array of perspectives held by different stakeholders is paramount. The challenges here are not just technical but deeply human. Each individual brings a unique set of experiences, biases, values, and expectations to the table, and these can significantly influence the project's trajectory.

When navigating through a toxic environment, it's essential to first recognize the root causes of toxicity. Often, these stem from unresolved conflicts, miscommunications, or entrenched power dynamics. By diving into the perspectives of each stakeholder, one can uncover underlying issues that may not be immediately apparent. For instance, a project manager might find that a team member's resistance to a particular task is not due to laziness or incompetence but rather a lack of clarity or previous negative experiences with similar tasks.

The key to managing these diverse perspectives lies in active listening. This goes beyond merely hearing words; it involves understanding the emotions and intentions behind them. In a toxic environment, people often feel unheard and undervalued, which exacerbates negative behaviors. A project manager who listens actively can identify these feelings and address them constructively. This might involve private one-on-one conversations where individuals feel safe to express their true thoughts without fear of retribution.

Empathy plays a crucial role in this process. By putting oneself in another's shoes, a project manager can better appreciate the pressures and motivations driving different behaviors. For example, a senior executive might be pushing for rapid progress due to external pressures from stakeholders or market conditions, while a team member might be advocating for a slower pace to ensure quality and avoid burnout. Understanding these differing pressures helps in finding a middle ground that respects both perspectives.

Cultural factors also significantly impact how perspectives are formed and communicated. In a multinational team, cultural misunderstandings can quickly lead to friction. What might be considered a straightforward directive in one culture can be perceived as rude or overbearing in another. Being aware of these cultural nuances and adjusting communication styles accordingly can mitigate misunderstandings and foster a more inclusive environment.

Conflict resolution is another critical aspect of managing diverse perspectives. In a toxic environment, conflicts are often more frequent and intense. A project manager must be adept at mediating disputes, ensuring that all parties feel heard, and working towards a resolution that everyone can accept. This requires patience, diplomacy, and a keen sense of fairness.

Moreover, transparency and consistency in decision-making help in managing expectations. When stakeholders understand the rationale behind decisions, even if they don't entirely agree with them, they are more likely to accept and support them. This transparency also builds trust, which is often lacking in toxic environments.

Finally, fostering a culture of mutual respect and collaboration can transform a toxic environment. Encouraging open dialogue, recognizing and valuing each individual's contributions, and creating opportunities for team members to share their perspectives can gradually shift the atmosphere from one of toxicity to one of cooperation and mutual respect.

By deeply understanding and valuing diverse perspectives, a project manager can navigate the complexities of toxic environments more effectively, turning potential pitfalls into opportunities for growth and improvement.

Inclusive Team Practices

Creating an inclusive team environment is fundamental for managing projects in toxic environments. In such settings, team dynamics can be strained, making it imperative to foster a culture that values every member's input and ensures that all voices are heard. This approach not only enhances team cohesion but also drives productivity and innovation, crucial for navigating the challenges inherent in toxic workspaces.

One of the first steps in cultivating inclusivity is recognizing and addressing unconscious biases. These biases can subtly influence decision-making and interactions, often leading to the marginalization of certain team members. Regular training sessions focused on bias awareness can help team members identify and mitigate these biases. This promotes a more equitable environment where everyone feels valued and respected.

Effective communication is another cornerstone of inclusive team practices. Encouraging open and honest dialogue helps in building trust and understanding among team members. Regular team meetings should be structured to allow everyone to contribute. This can be achieved by setting clear agendas, ensuring that quieter members have opportunities to speak, and actively soliciting diverse viewpoints. Utilizing various communication channels, such as face-to-face meetings, emails, and collaborative tools, can cater to different communication styles and preferences, further enhancing inclusivity.

Leadership plays a pivotal role in fostering an inclusive environment. Leaders must model inclusive behavior by actively listening to their team members, showing empathy, and being transparent in their decision-making processes. They should also be vigilant in recognizing and addressing any signs of exclusion or discrimination within the team. By doing so, leaders can create a safe space where team members feel comfortable sharing their ideas and concerns.

Diversity in team composition is another critical element. A diverse team brings a wide range of perspectives and experiences, which can be invaluable in problem-solving and innovation. When forming teams, it's essential to consider various dimensions of diversity, including but not limited to gender, ethnicity, age, and professional background. This diversity should not be superficial; it must be genuinely integrated into the team's fabric, ensuring that all members have equal opportunities to contribute and influence the project's direction.

Inclusive team practices also involve recognizing and celebrating the unique strengths and contributions of each team member.

Providing regular feedback and acknowledging achievements can boost morale and reinforce a sense of belonging. Additionally, offering professional development opportunities tailored to individual needs and aspirations can help team members feel valued and invested in the project's success.

Flexibility in work arrangements can further support inclusivity. In toxic environments, rigid structures can exacerbate stress and hinder productivity. Allowing flexible working hours, remote work options, and accommodating personal needs can help team members manage their work-life balance better. This flexibility demonstrates a commitment to their well-being and can lead to higher job satisfaction and retention.

Inclusive team practices are not a one-time effort but an ongoing commitment. Regularly assessing the team's inclusivity through surveys, feedback sessions, and performance metrics is essential. This continuous evaluation helps in identifying areas for improvement and ensures that the practices remain effective and relevant.

Incorporating these inclusive practices can transform a toxic environment into a more supportive and collaborative space. By valuing diversity, encouraging open communication, and providing strong leadership, teams can overcome the challenges posed by toxic environments and achieve their project goals more effectively.

Conflict and Diversity

Navigating the intricate maze of project management within toxic environments often requires a keen understanding of the underlying conflicts and the diversity that fuels them. These settings are rarely straightforward; they are composed of a tapestry of personalities, backgrounds, and competing interests that can either drive a project to success or to its knees. Recognizing and addressing these elements is crucial for any project manager aiming to maintain harmony and productivity.

Conflicts in toxic environments are not merely disagreements; they are often deeply rooted in a complex interplay of personal ambitions, historical grievances, and organizational politics. These conflicts can manifest in various ways, from overt confrontations to passive-aggressive behaviors and subtle undermining. It's essential to identify the sources of these conflicts early on. They might stem from unclear roles and responsibilities, resource limitations, or misaligned objectives. A project manager must act as a detective, peeling back the layers to understand the true origins of discord.

Diversity within a team, while a source of strength, can also be a breeding ground for misunderstandings and conflicts. Differences in cultural backgrounds, communication styles, and work ethics can lead to friction. However, these differences, if managed correctly, can also lead to innovative solutions and a more resilient project team. The key lies in fostering an environment where all voices are heard and respected. This involves not only formal mechanisms like regular team meetings and feedback sessions but also informal ones, such as team-building activities and open-door policies.

Effective communication is the lifeblood of managing conflicts and harnessing diversity. In toxic environments, communication channels are often clogged with misinformation, gossip, and a lack of transparency. A project manager must cut through this noise with clear, consistent, and honest communication. This includes setting the tone from the top, ensuring that all team members are on the same page regarding project goals, timelines, and expectations. It also means being an active listener, showing empathy, and addressing concerns promptly.

One of the most challenging aspects of managing projects in toxic environments is dealing with entrenched behaviors and attitudes. Toxic environments often have a history of unresolved issues and negative patterns that have become ingrained in the organizational culture. Changing these behaviors requires a strategic approach. It involves not only addressing the immediate issues but also working on long-term cultural change. This might include conflict resolution training, leadership development programs, and initiatives aimed at improving workplace morale and trust.

Building alliances and leveraging the strengths of diverse team members is another critical strategy. In a toxic environment, it's easy for project managers to feel isolated and overwhelmed. Forming alliances with key stakeholders, mentors, and even other project managers can provide much-needed support and perspective. Recognizing and utilizing the unique strengths of each team member can also turn diversity from a potential liability into a significant asset.

In the realm of project management, the ability to navigate conflicts and leverage diversity is a hallmark of effective leadership. Toxic environments, with their unique challenges, require a heightened level of awareness, empathy, and strategic thinking. By understanding the roots of conflicts, fostering inclusive communication, addressing entrenched behaviors, and building strong alliances, project managers can not only survive but thrive in these demanding settings. The journey is not easy, but the rewards—a cohesive, innovative, and high-performing team—are well worth the effort.

Harnessing Diverse Strengths

In the labyrinth of managing projects within toxic environments, the key to navigating through the myriad challenges often lies in the diverse strengths of the team. Picture a mosaic, each piece with its own unique color and shape, coming together to form a coherent picture. This is the essence of harnessing diverse strengths in a project team.

The first step involves recognizing the individual talents and skills each team member brings to the table. In a toxic environment, where negative dynamics can overshadow potential, it is crucial to see beyond the surface-level conflicts and identify the unique capabilities that can drive the project forward. For instance, a team member who excels in analytical thinking can be instrumental in breaking down complex problems into manageable tasks, while another who possesses strong interpersonal skills can facilitate communication and mediate conflicts.

Creating an environment where these diverse strengths can flourish requires deliberate effort. Leaders must foster a culture of inclusivity and respect, where every team member feels valued and heard. This can be achieved through regular team-building activities and open forums for discussion, where individuals are encouraged to share their ideas and perspectives.

By doing so, the team can leverage a wide range of viewpoints and approaches, leading to more innovative solutions and a richer project outcome.

Effective delegation is another cornerstone of harnessing diverse strengths. Assigning tasks based on individual strengths ensures that each team member is working in an area where they can excel. This not only boosts productivity but also enhances job satisfaction and morale, which are often in short supply in toxic environments. Moreover, it reduces the likelihood of burnout, as team members are more likely to be engaged and motivated when working on tasks that align with their skills and interests.

Communication is the lifeblood of any project, and it becomes even more critical in toxic environments. Establishing clear channels of communication, where information flows freely and transparently, helps in mitigating misunderstandings and conflicts. Regular check-ins and updates ensure that everyone is on the same page and can voice any concerns or suggestions. This open communication loop also allows for the continuous realignment of tasks and responsibilities, ensuring that the project remains on track and any issues are promptly addressed.

Mentorship and peer learning are powerful tools in harnessing diverse strengths. Pairing less experienced team members with seasoned professionals fosters a culture of continuous learning and growth. This not only helps in skill development but also strengthens the team's overall capability. In a toxic environment, where negativity can dampen enthusiasm, the positive influence of mentorship can be a beacon of support and encouragement.

Acknowledgment and celebration of individual and team achievements play a significant role in maintaining morale and motivation. Recognizing the contributions of each team member, no matter how small, creates a sense of accomplishment and reinforces the value of their unique strengths. In a toxic environment, where criticism often outweighs praise, such positive reinforcement can make a substantial difference in the team's dynamics and overall project success.

Harnessing diverse strengths is not merely a strategy but a necessity in managing projects within toxic environments. It requires a conscious effort to identify, cultivate, and leverage the unique capabilities of each team member. By doing so, leaders can transform a potentially destructive environment into one where creativity, collaboration, and resilience thrive, ultimately steering the project towards success.

Chapter 10: Case Studies of Success in Toxic Environments

Turnaround Stories

In the dimly lit corridors of corporate offices, where the air is thick with tension and the atmosphere is charged with uncertainty, the tales of project turnarounds are whispered like legends. These stories are not just about salvaging failing ventures but about navigating the treacherous waters of toxic environments where morale is low, trust is scarce, and stakes are high. The protagonists in these narratives are the unsung heroes of the corporate world—project managers who step into the fray with nothing but their wits, resilience, and an unyielding belief in the possibility of change.

Picture a project on the brink of collapse. Deadlines have been missed, budgets have been blown, and the team is fragmented, each member disillusioned and disengaged. The office, once buzzing with the excitement of a new venture, now feels oppressive, the weight of unmet expectations hanging heavy in the air. It's in this bleak setting that the turnaround stories begin, often with the arrival of a new project manager, someone who sees not just the problems but the potential solutions.

The first step in these stories is always about understanding the landscape. The new project manager takes the time to listen, to really hear the grievances and frustrations of the team members. This isn't just about gathering information; it's about building trust. In an environment where trust has been eroded, this simple act of listening can be revolutionary. It signals a change in leadership style, from dictatorial to collaborative, and begins to sow the seeds of hope.

Once the landscape is understood, the next phase involves identifying the root causes of the project's issues. This isn't a superficial analysis but a deep dive into the project's history, the decisions that were made, and the dynamics of the team. Often, the problems are not just technical but deeply human— miscommunications, lack of clarity, unrealistic expectations, and sometimes, personal conflicts. The project manager must wear many hats: detective, psychologist, mediator. Each problem uncovered is a step closer to the solution.

With a clear understanding of the issues, the project manager then turns to strategy. This is where the magic happens. Solutions are not one-size-fits-all; they must be tailored to the specific challenges and strengths of the team and the project. The strategy often involves restructuring the project plan, reallocating resources, and setting new, realistic goals. But more importantly, it involves re-energizing the team. The project manager must inspire, motivate, and lead by example. Small wins are celebrated to build momentum, and setbacks are treated as learning opportunities rather than failures.

Communication becomes the lifeblood of the turnaround. Transparent, frequent, and honest communication helps rebuild trust and keeps everyone aligned. The project manager creates a culture where feedback is welcomed, and contributions are valued. This cultural shift is crucial; it transforms a toxic environment into a fertile ground for innovation and collaboration.

As the project begins to stabilize, the changes become evident. Deadlines are met, quality improves, and the team starts to function as a cohesive unit. The office, once a place of dread, becomes a hive of activity and purpose. The turnaround is not just about saving a project; it's about transforming an environment and unlocking the potential of the people within it.

These stories serve as powerful reminders that even in the most toxic environments, change is possible. They highlight the importance of leadership, empathy, and strategic thinking in managing projects. Through these narratives, we learn that the true essence of project management lies not just in managing tasks but in leading people through adversity to success.

Lessons from the Field

Seasoned project managers often find themselves navigating the treacherous waters of toxic work environments, where negativity, resistance, and dysfunction are the norms rather than exceptions. These environments can be challenging, but they also offer invaluable lessons that can transform a manager's approach to leading projects.

Observing the dynamics in such settings reveals a tapestry of human behaviors. Teams in toxic environments frequently operate under a cloud of mistrust and low morale. Communication breakdowns are common, leading to misunderstandings and conflicts. The pressure cooker atmosphere often results in high turnover rates, as employees seek refuge from the stress and frustration. Yet, amidst this chaos, there are patterns and strategies that can be discerned and harnessed.

One of the first lessons from the field is the critical importance of establishing trust. In toxic environments, trust is often the first casualty. Rebuilding it requires transparency and consistency. Project managers must be forthright in their communications, setting clear expectations and following through on promises. This fosters an atmosphere where team members feel secure enough to voice their concerns and ideas without fear of retribution.

Another key lesson is the power of empathy. Toxic environments can leave individuals feeling undervalued and unheard. By actively listening and showing genuine concern for their well-being, project managers can create a buffer against the negativity. Empathy bridges the gap between leadership and team members, fostering a sense of unity and shared purpose.

Navigating these environments also demands a keen understanding of organizational politics. Toxic workplaces are often rife with power struggles and hidden agendas. A savvy project manager must be adept at reading these undercurrents and maneuvering through them without becoming entangled. This involves building alliances and leveraging influence strategically to advance the project's goals while minimizing resistance.

Flexibility is another crucial attribute. In a toxic environment, rigidity can be a project's downfall. Adaptability allows a project manager to pivot in response to unexpected challenges and shifting priorities. This agility not only keeps the project on track but also demonstrates resilience and resourcefulness to the team, which can be inspiring and motivating.

Managing stress is an indispensable skill gleaned from these environments. Toxic workplaces are breeding grounds for stress, which can cripple productivity and creativity. Effective project managers develop techniques to mitigate stress, both for themselves and their teams. This might involve implementing regular check-ins, fostering a supportive team culture, or providing resources for mental health.

Finally, maintaining a focus on the end goal is essential. Toxic environments can easily distract and demoralize, but a clear vision of the project's objectives can serve as a beacon. Project managers must continually remind their teams of the bigger picture, celebrating small victories along the way to maintain momentum and morale.

These lessons, hard-earned in the crucible of toxic environments, equip project managers with a robust toolkit. They emerge more resilient, empathetic, and strategic, ready to tackle the most daunting of projects with a newfound confidence and insight.

Innovative Solutions

Navigating the murky waters of toxic environments requires more than just traditional project management techniques. It demands creativity, resilience, and a willingness to explore unconventional solutions. The landscape is often riddled with obstacles that can derail even the most meticulously planned projects. These challenges range from interpersonal conflicts and political maneuvering to resource constraints and shifting priorities. In such settings, innovative solutions become not just advantageous, but essential.

One key approach is leveraging technology to bridge gaps and streamline processes. Advanced project management software, for instance, can offer real-time updates, facilitate transparent communication, and provide data-driven insights. These tools can help mitigate the risks associated with miscommunication and misalignment, which are common in toxic environments. By utilizing platforms that foster collaboration and accountability, project managers can create a more cohesive and motivated team dynamic, even when underlying tensions exist.

Another strategy involves fostering a culture of psychological safety. Toxic environments often breed fear and anxiety, which stifle creativity and innovation. By prioritizing open communication and encouraging team members to voice their concerns without fear of retribution, project managers can tap into a wealth of untapped potential. Techniques such as regular feedback loops, anonymous suggestion boxes, and dedicated conflict resolution sessions can be instrumental in this regard.

Creating a safe space for dialogue can uncover hidden issues and pave the way for innovative problem-solving.

Resourcefulness is another critical component. In toxic environments, resources are often limited or misallocated. Project managers must think outside the box to make the most of what they have. This might involve repurposing existing assets, forming strategic alliances, or seeking out alternative funding sources. Crowdsourcing ideas and solutions from within the team can also yield surprising and effective results. When team members feel empowered to contribute their unique perspectives, it can lead to creative and resource-efficient solutions.

Flexibility and adaptability are also crucial. Toxic environments are often characterized by volatility and unpredictability. Rigid plans and processes can quickly become obsolete. Agile methodologies, which emphasize iterative progress and continuous improvement, can be particularly effective in such settings. By breaking projects into smaller, manageable chunks and regularly reassessing priorities, project managers can remain responsive to changing circumstances. This approach not only helps in navigating immediate challenges but also builds a resilient and adaptable team.

Leadership plays a pivotal role in driving innovation in toxic environments. A leader who leads by example, demonstrating resilience, integrity, and a commitment to the team's well-being, can inspire others to follow suit. Transparent decision-making, recognition of efforts, and a clear vision can galvanize a team, even in the face of adversity. Leaders who are willing to take calculated risks and embrace unconventional solutions can set a powerful precedent for the entire team.

Lastly, continuous learning and development should be encouraged. Toxic environments can be draining, but they also offer unique learning opportunities. By fostering a mindset of growth and continuous improvement, project managers can turn challenges into learning experiences. This might involve formal training programs, mentorship, or simply creating opportunities for team members to step outside their comfort zones and take on new responsibilities.

In essence, managing projects in toxic environments requires a multifaceted approach. It involves leveraging technology, fostering psychological safety, being resourceful, staying flexible, demonstrating strong leadership, and promoting continuous learning. By embracing these innovative solutions, project managers can not only navigate the complexities of toxic environments but also transform them into opportunities for growth and success.

Sustaining Long-Term Success

In the ever-evolving landscape of project management, ensuring long-term success in toxic environments demands a multifaceted approach. Toxic environments, characterized by poor communication, low morale, and high stress, can significantly derail even the most meticulously planned projects. To sustain long-term success, it is essential to cultivate resilience, adaptability, and a culture of continuous improvement.

One critical aspect of sustaining long-term success is fostering a resilient team. Resilience is the capacity to recover quickly from difficulties, and in a toxic environment, it is a vital trait for any project team. Building resilience involves providing support systems, such as access to mental health resources and stress management workshops. Regular team-building activities and open forums for discussion can also help in strengthening team bonds and creating a supportive atmosphere. Encouraging a work-life balance and recognizing individual contributions can further enhance team morale, making the group more capable of weathering challenges.

Adaptability is another cornerstone of long-term success in toxic environments. Projects rarely go exactly as planned, and the ability to pivot and adjust strategies is crucial. This requires a flexible project management framework that can accommodate changes without causing significant disruptions. Agile methodologies, for instance, are particularly effective in such settings. They promote iterative progress and constant feedback, allowing teams to make adjustments in real-time. Regular training and development programs can equip team members with the skills needed to adapt to new technologies, processes, and market demands.

A culture of continuous improvement is indispensable for sustaining long-term success. This involves regularly reviewing and refining processes, tools, and approaches to ensure they remain effective and relevant. Implementing a robust feedback mechanism where team members can share insights and suggestions can lead to meaningful improvements. Conducting regular retrospectives can help identify areas of improvement and celebrate successes, fostering a mindset of growth and development. Encouraging innovation and experimentation can also drive continuous improvement, as it allows teams to explore new ideas and solutions without fear of failure.

Effective communication is a linchpin in managing projects in toxic environments. Clear, transparent, and consistent communication can mitigate misunderstandings and reduce the potential for conflicts. Establishing regular check-ins and updates can keep everyone aligned and informed about project progress and any changes. Utilizing collaboration tools and platforms can facilitate better communication and ensure that information is easily accessible to all team members. Active listening and empathetic communication can also help in addressing concerns and building trust within the team.

Leadership plays a pivotal role in sustaining long-term success in toxic environments. Leaders must exemplify the values and behaviors they wish to see in their teams. This includes demonstrating integrity, accountability, and a commitment to the well-being of the team. Providing clear direction and setting realistic expectations can help in managing stress and preventing burnout. Leaders should also be proactive in addressing toxic behaviors and fostering an inclusive, respectful, and positive work culture.

Monitoring and measuring progress is essential for sustaining long-term success. Implementing key performance indicators (KPIs) and regular progress reviews can help in tracking the project's trajectory and identifying potential issues early on. Utilizing project management software and tools can streamline this process and provide valuable insights into team performance and project health. Regularly assessing risks and developing contingency plans can also ensure that the project remains on track despite unforeseen challenges.

Sustaining long-term success in toxic environments is a complex and ongoing endeavor. It requires a holistic approach that addresses the well-being of the team, the adaptability of processes, and the effectiveness of communication. By fostering resilience, promoting adaptability, nurturing a culture of continuous improvement, ensuring effective communication, demonstrating strong leadership, and monitoring progress, project managers can navigate the challenges of toxic environments and achieve enduring success.

Chapter 11: Tools and Techniques for Managing Toxicity

Diagnostic Tools

Within the realm of project management, especially in challenging and toxic environments, the ability to diagnose issues accurately and promptly is paramount. Diagnostic tools serve as the first line of defense, offering insights into the health of a project and highlighting areas that demand immediate attention. These tools, when aptly employed, can transform a chaotic situation into a manageable one by providing clarity and direction.

The cornerstone of effective diagnostics in project management is the identification of key performance indicators (KPIs). KPIs are quantifiable measures that gauge the success of a project against its objectives. In toxic environments, where uncertainty and volatility are common, KPIs must be meticulously chosen to reflect both the strategic goals and the operational realities. Common KPIs include budget variance, schedule adherence, resource utilization, and stakeholder satisfaction. These indicators, when tracked consistently, can reveal trends and patterns that might otherwise go unnoticed.

Another crucial diagnostic tool is the SWOT analysis, which stands for Strengths, Weaknesses, Opportunities, and Threats. This framework allows project managers to assess the internal and external factors that could impact the project's success. In toxic environments, where external threats might be more pronounced and internal weaknesses more debilitating, a thorough SWOT analysis can provide a balanced view of the project landscape. By identifying strengths, managers can leverage them to counteract weaknesses. Recognizing opportunities can help in navigating threats more effectively.

Risk assessment matrices are indispensable in environments fraught with uncertainty. These matrices help in identifying, evaluating, and prioritizing risks based on their likelihood and impact. In toxic settings, risks are often multifaceted and dynamic, necessitating a robust and flexible approach. By regularly updating the risk assessment matrix, project managers can stay ahead of potential issues and devise contingency plans. This proactive stance not only mitigates risks but also instills confidence among stakeholders.

Stakeholder analysis is another vital diagnostic tool. Understanding the needs, expectations, and influence of various stakeholders can significantly affect a project's trajectory. In toxic environments, stakeholder dynamics are often complex and fluid. A comprehensive stakeholder analysis helps in mapping out these relationships and identifying key influencers. By engaging stakeholders effectively, project managers can foster a collaborative atmosphere even in the most challenging scenarios.

Earned Value Management (EVM) is a sophisticated diagnostic tool that integrates project scope, schedule, and cost variables. EVM provides a quantitative measure of project performance and progress. In toxic environments, where deviations from the plan are more likely, EVM can offer early warnings of potential issues. By comparing planned progress with actual progress, project managers can identify variances and take corrective actions promptly.

Communication audits are essential for diagnosing issues related to information flow within the project team and with external stakeholders. In toxic environments, miscommunication is a common pitfall that can exacerbate existing problems. Regular communication audits help in identifying gaps, redundancies, and bottlenecks in the communication process. By addressing these issues, project managers can ensure that information is disseminated accurately and timely, thereby reducing misunderstandings and conflicts.

Lastly, health checks or project audits provide a comprehensive review of the project's status at regular intervals. These audits examine various aspects such as compliance with standards, alignment with objectives, and adherence to processes. In toxic environments, where conditions can deteriorate rapidly, regular health checks are crucial for maintaining control and ensuring the project remains on track.

Diagnostic tools, when used effectively, can illuminate the path forward in even the most toxic of project environments. They provide the necessary insights and data to make informed decisions, enabling project managers to navigate challenges with confidence and precision.

Intervention Strategies

In the realm of managing projects in toxic environments, the necessity for effective intervention strategies cannot be overstated. When navigating such challenging landscapes, it is paramount to employ a variety of tactical approaches designed to mitigate the adverse effects of toxicity and maintain project momentum.

At the core of these strategies lies the importance of clear and transparent communication. Establishing open channels for dialogue ensures that team members feel heard and understood, which can significantly reduce misunderstandings and conflicts. Regular check-ins and feedback sessions create a structured environment where issues can be addressed promptly, preventing them from escalating into larger problems.

Another critical strategy involves setting and maintaining clear boundaries. In toxic environments, it is easy for project scopes to become muddled and for responsibilities to overlap unproductively. By defining roles and responsibilities with precision, project managers can foster a sense of accountability and clarity among team members. This clarity helps in minimizing the stress and confusion that often accompany toxic work settings.

Conflict resolution techniques are indispensable tools in the intervention arsenal. Training team members in conflict resolution skills, such as active listening and empathy, can transform potential flashpoints into opportunities for growth and understanding. Mediation sessions, facilitated by an impartial third party, can also be highly effective in resolving deep-seated issues that impede project progress.

Building a supportive team culture is another essential strategy. Encouraging collaboration and mutual support among team members can counteract the isolating effects of a toxic environment. Team-building activities, both formal and informal, can strengthen interpersonal relationships and promote a sense of unity and collective purpose.

Moreover, it is crucial to recognize and address the sources of toxicity within the environment. This may involve identifying specific individuals or systemic issues that contribute to the negative atmosphere. Once identified, targeted interventions such as coaching, counseling, or even restructuring can be implemented to address these root causes. In some cases, it may be necessary to make difficult decisions, such as reassigning or removing individuals who perpetuate toxic behaviors.

Empowerment and autonomy also play significant roles in intervention strategies. Allowing team members to take ownership of their tasks and make decisions within their areas of expertise can boost morale and reduce feelings of helplessness. Providing opportunities for professional development and growth can further enhance their sense of value and engagement with the project.

Furthermore, fostering resilience within the team is vital. Equipping team members with stress management and coping techniques can help them navigate the pressures of a toxic environment more effectively. Workshops on mindfulness, time management, and work-life balance can provide practical tools for maintaining well-being and productivity.

Lastly, it is essential to maintain a focus on the long-term health of the project and the team. Regularly reassessing the intervention strategies and their effectiveness ensures that they remain relevant and impactful. Flexibility and adaptability are key, as the dynamics of toxic environments can change rapidly, requiring continuous vigilance and adjustment.

Through the implementation of these intervention strategies, project managers can create a more manageable and productive atmosphere, even within the most challenging environments. By prioritizing communication, clarity, conflict resolution, support, empowerment, and resilience, they can steer their projects towards successful outcomes despite the inherent difficulties.

Monitoring Progress

Keeping a vigilant eye on the progress of a project in a toxic environment requires a unique blend of precision, empathy, and adaptability. It is not simply about tracking milestones and deliverables; it is about understanding the subtle undercurrents that can derail even the most meticulously planned projects. The atmosphere in such environments can be laden with distrust, miscommunication, and hidden agendas. Effective monitoring, therefore, becomes an exercise in balancing technical oversight with acute emotional intelligence.

One of the first steps in monitoring progress is establishing clear, transparent metrics that all team members understand and agree upon. These metrics serve as the backbone of the project's progress tracking, providing objective data points that can be referenced in discussions and evaluations. However, in a toxic environment, the clarity of these metrics can often be clouded by misinterpretations or deliberate misinformation. It is essential to ensure that these metrics are not only communicated effectively but also reinforced through regular, open dialogue.

Regular check-ins and updates are crucial. These sessions should be designed to foster an atmosphere of openness and trust, where team members feel safe to express concerns and highlight issues without fear of retribution. The frequency and format of these check-ins may vary depending on the project's nature and the team's dynamics, but consistency is key. These meetings are not merely about reporting progress; they are opportunities to gauge the team's morale, identify potential red flags, and recalibrate strategies as needed.

In addition to formal meetings, informal interactions play a significant role in monitoring progress. Casual conversations, whether in person or through digital communication channels, can provide insights that might not surface in structured settings. These interactions help in understanding the unspoken issues that might be affecting the team's performance. Leaders must cultivate an approachable demeanor, encouraging team members to share their thoughts and feelings candidly.

Technology can be a powerful ally in monitoring progress. Project management tools and software provide real-time updates and analytics, offering a clear picture of where the project stands at any given moment. However, in a toxic environment, technology should be used cautiously. Over-reliance on digital tools can sometimes exacerbate feelings of surveillance and mistrust among team members. It is important to strike a balance where technology aids transparency and efficiency without undermining the human element.

Conflict resolution is another critical aspect of monitoring progress in a toxic environment. Disputes and disagreements are inevitable, but how they are managed can significantly impact the project's trajectory. Leaders must be adept at identifying the root causes of conflicts and addressing them constructively. This often involves mediating discussions, facilitating compromises, and ensuring that all voices are heard and respected. Effective conflict resolution not only keeps the project on track but also helps in building a more resilient and cohesive team.

Feedback loops are essential for continuous improvement. Constructive feedback should flow in all directions - from leaders to team members, among peers, and from the team back to the leadership. This feedback should be specific, actionable, and delivered in a manner that is both respectful and encouraging. In toxic environments, feedback can sometimes be weaponized, leading to further discord. It is crucial to establish a culture where feedback is seen as a tool for growth rather than a means of criticism.

Monitoring progress in toxic environments demands a delicate balance of vigilance, empathy, and strategic foresight. It is about creating a framework that not only tracks the tangible aspects of the project but also addresses the intangible elements that influence team dynamics and overall success. Through clear communication, regular check-ins, effective use of technology, conflict resolution, and constructive feedback, leaders can navigate the complexities of such environments and steer their projects towards successful completion.

Continuous Improvement

In the realm of project management, particularly within toxic environments, the concept of continuous improvement serves as a lifeline. It is the process of relentlessly seeking methods to enhance the efficiency, effectiveness, and quality of project outcomes. This practice is not merely a set of guidelines but a philosophy ingrained in every stage of the project lifecycle. In toxic environments, where challenges are abundant, continuous improvement becomes even more critical. It offers a structured approach to navigating the myriad of obstacles that can derail projects.

The first step in fostering a culture of continuous improvement is to recognize the importance of feedback. Feedback, when used constructively, provides invaluable insights into what is working and what is not. In toxic environments, feedback must be handled delicately to avoid exacerbating tensions. Establishing anonymous feedback channels can encourage honest communication without fear of retribution. Regularly scheduled debriefings and retrospectives allow team members to voice their concerns and suggest improvements in a structured manner. This not only aids in identifying issues but also in fostering a sense of ownership and collaboration among team members.

Data-driven decision-making is another cornerstone of continuous improvement. Collecting and analyzing data throughout the project can reveal patterns and trends that might not be immediately apparent. Key performance indicators (KPIs) should be established at the project's outset, and these metrics need to be monitored consistently. In toxic environments, where emotions and biases can cloud judgment, relying on empirical data helps maintain objectivity. It allows project managers to make informed decisions and adjustments, ensuring that the project remains aligned with its goals.

Training and development are essential components in the pursuit of continuous improvement. Investing in the professional growth of team members not only enhances their skills but also demonstrates a commitment to their well-being. In toxic environments, where morale can be low, offering opportunities for learning and advancement can be a powerful motivator. Workshops, seminars, and certifications related to project management and technical skills can equip the team with new tools and techniques. This continuous learning cycle fosters innovation and adaptability, both of which are crucial in navigating toxic environments.

Process optimization is another key aspect. Regularly reviewing and refining processes can lead to significant improvements in efficiency and effectiveness. This involves mapping out current processes, identifying bottlenecks, and implementing changes to streamline workflows. In toxic environments, where resources are often stretched thin, optimizing processes can alleviate some of the pressure. It ensures that the team is working smarter, not harder, and that resources are being utilized in the most effective manner possible.

The role of leadership in continuous improvement cannot be overstated. Leaders must set the tone by exemplifying a commitment to excellence and a willingness to adapt. They should encourage a culture where mistakes are viewed as learning opportunities rather than failures. In toxic environments, this mindset shift can be transformative. It reduces the fear of blame and fosters a more open and innovative atmosphere. Leaders should also be proactive in recognizing and rewarding improvements, no matter how small. Acknowledging progress reinforces the value of continuous improvement and motivates the team to keep striving for better outcomes.

In essence, continuous improvement in project management within toxic environments is about creating a resilient and adaptive framework. It involves leveraging feedback, data, training, process optimization, and strong leadership to navigate challenges and drive success. This approach not only enhances project outcomes but also contributes to a healthier, more collaborative work environment.

Chapter 12: Legal and Ethical Considerations

Understanding Legal Frameworks

Navigating the complexities of project management in toxic environments necessitates a thorough understanding of the legal frameworks that govern these challenging landscapes. Legal frameworks serve as the backbone for operational procedures, providing a structured pathway to ensure compliance, mitigate risk, and safeguard all stakeholders involved. They encompass a broad spectrum of regulations, statutes, and guidelines that are often specific to the industry, geographical location, and nature of the project.

In toxic environments, legal frameworks become even more critical due to the heightened risks and potential for severe consequences. These environments are often characterized by hazardous materials, stringent safety regulations, and heightened scrutiny from regulatory bodies. Understanding these legal parameters is not just a matter of compliance but a fundamental aspect of project planning and execution.

The first step in grasping legal frameworks is recognizing the key regulatory agencies and their mandates. Agencies such as the

Environmental Protection Agency (EPA), Occupational Safety and Health Administration (OSHA), and equivalent bodies in other countries set forth regulations that dictate how projects must be managed to protect both the environment and human health. Familiarizing oneself with the specific requirements and guidelines issued by these agencies is essential for any project manager operating in toxic environments.

Moreover, legal frameworks often include detailed procedures for handling hazardous materials. These procedures cover everything from the proper storage and transportation of dangerous substances to emergency response protocols in case of spills or accidental releases. Adhering to these guidelines not only ensures legal compliance but also minimizes the risk of catastrophic incidents that can lead to severe environmental damage, health hazards, and substantial financial penalties.

Contracts and agreements form another critical component of legal frameworks. These documents delineate the responsibilities, liabilities, and expectations of all parties involved in the project. In toxic environments, contracts often contain specialized clauses that address the unique risks and regulatory requirements associated with hazardous operations. Understanding and negotiating these terms is crucial for protecting the interests of the project and ensuring that all parties are clear on their obligations.

Insurance and liability are also pivotal aspects of legal frameworks in toxic environments. Given the high-risk nature of these projects, securing adequate insurance coverage is imperative. This includes not only general liability insurance but also specialized policies that cover environmental liabilities and workers' compensation. Understanding the scope and limitations of these insurance policies helps in planning for contingencies and managing potential legal exposures.

Documentation and reporting are integral to maintaining compliance with legal frameworks. Regulatory bodies often require detailed records of all activities related to the project, including safety inspections, incident reports, and environmental impact assessments. Maintaining thorough and accurate documentation ensures that the project can withstand regulatory scrutiny and provides a clear record in the event of disputes or legal challenges.

Lastly, ongoing education and training are essential for staying abreast of changes in legal frameworks. Regulations and standards evolve, and staying informed about these changes is vital for ensuring continuous compliance. Regular training sessions for project teams and staying connected with industry associations can provide valuable updates and insights into new legal requirements and best practices.

Understanding legal frameworks in toxic environments is a multifaceted endeavor that demands attention to detail, proactive planning, and continuous education. It is the foundation upon which safe, compliant, and successful project management is built, ensuring that all activities are conducted within the bounds of the law and in a manner that protects both people and the planet.

Ethical Decision Making

Navigating the treacherous waters of project management in toxic environments necessitates a robust framework for making ethical decisions. This becomes even more critical when the very nature of the environment challenges one's moral compass. Ethical decision-making is not merely a matter of adhering to a set of rules but involves a profound understanding of the implications of one's actions on various stakeholders.

In toxic environments, where the pressure to deliver results often supersedes the means of achieving them, project managers face dilemmas that test their ethical boundaries. The key is to develop a keen sense of ethical awareness, which involves recognizing the potential for harm, understanding the vested interests of all parties involved, and weighing the long-term consequences of decisions. This requires a balance between organizational goals and the well-being of the team, clients, and the broader community.

One of the primary challenges in these settings is the prevalence of unethical practices that may be normalized. Whether it is cutting corners, misrepresenting progress, or neglecting the welfare of team members, the toxic culture can create an environment where unethical behavior is not just tolerated but expected. Project managers must resist the temptation to conform and instead cultivate a culture of integrity. This involves setting clear ethical standards, modeling ethical behavior, and fostering an environment where ethical considerations are part of the decision-making process.

Transparency plays a critical role in ethical decision-making. Open communication channels ensure that all stakeholders are aware of the project's progress and any issues that arise. This openness helps build trust and facilitates a collaborative approach to problem-solving. It also means being honest about potential risks and challenges, rather than glossing over them to present a falsely optimistic outlook. Ethical project managers prioritize truthfulness, even when it is uncomfortable or may lead to difficult conversations.

Another essential aspect is accountability. In toxic environments, there is often a lack of accountability, with blame-shifting and scapegoating being common tactics. Ethical project managers take responsibility for their actions and decisions. They create mechanisms for accountability within their teams, ensuring that everyone understands their roles and the ethical standards they are expected to uphold. This not only helps in maintaining ethical integrity but also empowers team members to act ethically, knowing that their actions are supported by a framework of accountability.

Decision-making frameworks, such as utilitarianism, deontology, and virtue ethics, can provide valuable guidance in navigating ethical dilemmas. Utilitarianism focuses on the greatest good for the greatest number, while deontology emphasizes duties and rules. Virtue ethics, on the other hand, considers the character and virtues of the decision-maker. By applying these frameworks, project managers can systematically evaluate their options and make informed ethical decisions.

Ethical decision-making is an ongoing process that requires continuous reflection and adaptation. Project managers must remain vigilant and be willing to reassess their decisions in light of new information or changing circumstances. This dynamic approach ensures that ethical considerations are not static but evolve with the project and its environment.

Developing an ethical approach to project management in toxic environments is undoubtedly challenging. It requires courage, conviction, and a commitment to doing what is right, even in the face of adversity. By prioritizing ethical decision-making, project managers can navigate the complexities of toxic environments, fostering a culture of integrity that ultimately leads to more sustainable and successful project outcomes.

Handling Grievances

Dealing with grievances in a toxic project environment requires a nuanced approach that balances empathy with assertiveness. The first step is recognizing the signs of discontent among team members. Often, grievances manifest as reduced productivity, increased absenteeism, or a palpable tension in the workplace. Identifying these early signs is crucial for addressing issues before they escalate.

Listening is a critical skill in handling grievances. Create an open-door policy where team members feel safe to voice their concerns. This involves not only making time for these conversations but also actively listening without interrupting. Acknowledge their feelings and validate their experiences, even if you do not immediately agree with their perspective.

Once a grievance is aired, it is essential to document the complaint in detail. This documentation should include the nature of the grievance, the parties involved, and any specific incidents cited. This record serves as a reference point for any future discussions and ensures that there is an accurate account of the issue at hand.

After understanding the grievance, the next step is to investigate. This involves gathering information from all relevant parties and reviewing any pertinent documentation. The goal is to get a comprehensive view of the situation. It is important to approach this investigation impartially, avoiding any preconceived notions or biases.

Effective communication plays a pivotal role throughout this process. Keep the complainant informed about the steps being taken to address their grievance. Transparency helps build trust and demonstrates that their concerns are being taken seriously. However, be cautious about sharing sensitive information that could exacerbate the situation or breach confidentiality.

In toxic environments, grievances often stem from deeper systemic issues. Therefore, addressing a grievance may require more than just resolving a specific complaint. It may necessitate broader changes to the project's management practices, team dynamics, or organizational culture. Engage in a root cause analysis to identify underlying problems and develop strategies to mitigate them.

Conflict resolution techniques can be invaluable in handling grievances. Mediation, for instance, can be an effective way to facilitate a constructive dialogue between conflicting parties. A neutral mediator can help clarify misunderstandings, encourage empathy, and guide the parties towards a mutually agreeable solution. Alternatively, arbitration might be necessary for more complex or severe disputes.

It is also important to establish clear policies and procedures for handling grievances. These should outline the steps for filing a complaint, the investigation process, and the potential outcomes. Having a structured approach ensures consistency and fairness in how grievances are managed.

Training managers and team leaders on how to handle grievances is equally crucial. Equip them with the skills to recognize early signs of discontent, engage in active listening, and facilitate conflict resolution. Regular training sessions can help reinforce these skills and keep them updated on best practices.

Monitoring the resolution of grievances is the final step. Follow up with the complainant to ensure that the solution implemented is effective and that the issue has been adequately resolved. This follow-up demonstrates a commitment to maintaining a healthy work environment and helps prevent the recurrence of similar issues.

Managing grievances in toxic environments is a challenging but essential aspect of project management. It requires a proactive, empathetic, and systematic approach to ensure that team members feel heard, valued, and supported. By addressing grievances effectively, project managers can foster a more positive and productive working environment.

Protecting Whistleblowers

Whistleblowers play a crucial role in identifying and exposing unethical practices and toxic behaviors within organizations. Ensuring their protection is of paramount importance, especially in environments where retaliation can be swift and severe. A project's success can hinge on the integrity of its processes, and whistleblowers often stand as the last line of defense against the erosion of this integrity.

Creating a culture where whistleblowers feel safe to report wrongdoing begins with clear policies and procedures. Organizations must establish comprehensive whistleblowing policies that outline the steps for reporting concerns, the protections available to whistleblowers, and the consequences for retaliating against them. These policies should be easily accessible and communicated regularly to all employees to reinforce the organization's commitment to ethical behavior.

Confidentiality is a cornerstone of effective whistleblower protection. When individuals come forward with sensitive information, they must trust that their identity will be protected to the fullest extent possible. This means implementing secure channels for reporting, such as anonymous hotlines or encrypted email systems, and limiting access to whistleblower identities to only those who need to know to investigate the claim.

Training is another critical component in protecting whistleblowers. Employees at all levels should receive regular training on the importance of whistleblowing, how to report concerns, and the protections in place for those who do so. This training should also emphasize the organization's zero-tolerance policy for retaliation, making it clear that any form of retribution against whistleblowers will be met with serious consequences.

Leadership plays a pivotal role in fostering an environment where whistleblowers feel safe and supported. Leaders must model ethical behavior and demonstrate a genuine commitment to transparency and accountability. They should actively encourage employees to speak up about concerns and provide visible support to those who do. When leaders take whistleblower reports seriously and act promptly to address issues, it sends a powerful message that the organization values integrity and will protect those who uphold it.

In addition to internal measures, organizations should be aware of external protections available to whistleblowers. Many countries have laws that provide legal safeguards for whistleblowers, including protections against dismissal, demotion, and other forms of retaliation. Being knowledgeable about these laws and ensuring that the organization's policies align with them can provide additional layers of protection for whistleblowers.

Investigations into whistleblower claims must be thorough, impartial, and conducted with the utmost discretion. The process should be transparent, with clear timelines and communication about the steps being taken. Whistleblowers should be informed of the progress and outcomes of investigations, reinforcing their trust in the system and the organization's commitment to addressing their concerns.

Support mechanisms for whistleblowers are also essential. Offering counseling services, legal advice, and other forms of support can help mitigate the personal and professional stress that often accompanies whistleblowing. By providing these resources, organizations demonstrate a holistic approach to protecting and supporting whistleblowers, recognizing the significant personal risks they take in coming forward.

Ultimately, protecting whistleblowers is not just about compliance with laws and policies; it's about fostering a culture of integrity, transparency, and accountability. When organizations prioritize the protection of whistleblowers, they not only safeguard individuals but also strengthen the ethical foundations of their operations, paving the way for more successful and sustainable project outcomes.

Chapter 13: Creating a Sustainable Positive Environment

Long-Term Cultural Change

The environment within which a project operates can have profound effects on its success or failure. In settings characterized by toxicity, the challenges are amplified, making it crucial to address the underlying cultural issues. The roots of a toxic environment often run deep, manifesting in entrenched behaviors, attitudes, and practices that can stymie progress and innovation. Shifting this deep-seated culture requires a sustained and strategic approach, focusing on long-term change rather than quick fixes.

At the heart of cultural transformation is the recognition that culture is not static; it evolves over time through the interactions and behaviors of individuals within the organization. Therefore, the first step involves a thorough understanding of the existing cultural dynamics. This can be achieved through comprehensive assessments, such as surveys, interviews, and observational studies, to identify specific toxic elements and their origins. These insights provide a foundation upon which to build a strategy for change.

Leadership plays a pivotal role in driving cultural change. Leaders must not only advocate for change but also embody the desired cultural attributes. Their actions, decisions, and interactions set the tone for the entire organization. By demonstrating commitment to new values and behaviors, leaders can inspire others to follow suit. This often involves transparent communication about the reasons for change, the benefits it will bring, and the steps involved in the transformation process.

Creating a vision for the future is another critical aspect. This vision should be compelling and clearly articulated, providing a sense of direction and purpose. It should outline the desired cultural attributes and how they align with the organization's goals and values. Engaging employees in the development of this vision can foster a sense of ownership and commitment, making them active participants in the change process.

Training and development programs are essential tools for equipping employees with the skills and knowledge needed to thrive in the new cultural landscape. These programs should focus not only on technical skills but also on soft skills such as communication, collaboration, and conflict resolution. By fostering these competencies, organizations can create a more supportive and cohesive work environment.

Reinforcement mechanisms are crucial for sustaining cultural change. This can include revising policies, procedures, and reward systems to align with the new cultural attributes. For instance, performance evaluations and promotions should reflect the desired behaviors and values, sending a clear message about what is valued within the organization. Regular feedback and recognition can also reinforce positive behaviors and motivate employees to continue supporting the cultural shift.

Monitoring and evaluation are integral to the change process. Regular assessments can help track progress, identify areas for improvement, and ensure that the change efforts are on the right path. This can involve both quantitative measures, such as employee surveys and performance metrics, and qualitative feedback, such as focus groups and interviews. By continually assessing the impact of the change initiatives, organizations can make necessary adjustments and maintain momentum.

Cultural change is inherently complex and requires patience and persistence. It involves altering deeply ingrained habits and mindsets, which can be met with resistance. However, by taking a strategic, inclusive, and sustained approach, organizations can navigate these challenges and create a healthier, more productive work environment. This not only enhances the success of individual projects but also contributes to the overall resilience and adaptability of the organization.

Leadership Development

Developing effective leadership is crucial for navigating the complexities of toxic work environments. Leaders in such settings face unique challenges that require a blend of resilience, empathy, and strategic acumen. The ability to inspire and manage a team under duress is not an innate skill but one that can be honed through deliberate practice and thoughtful development.

Effective leadership begins with self-awareness. Leaders must first understand their own strengths, weaknesses, and triggers. This introspection allows them to manage their reactions and maintain composure in the face of adversity. Self-aware leaders are better equipped to foster a positive atmosphere, even when external conditions are less than ideal. They can identify stress points within themselves and their teams, addressing issues before they escalate into larger problems.

Emotional intelligence is another critical component. Leaders who can empathize with their team members build trust and loyalty. In toxic environments, where morale is often low, the ability to connect on a human level can be a powerful antidote to negativity. Leaders should actively listen to their team, validate their experiences, and offer support. This creates a sense of safety and belonging, which can mitigate the damaging effects of a toxic workplace.

Communication skills are paramount. Clear, transparent, and consistent communication helps to manage expectations and reduce uncertainties. Leaders should provide regular updates, openly discuss challenges, and involve their team in problem-solving processes. This not only keeps everyone informed but also empowers team members by giving them a sense of control and participation.

Strategic thinking is essential for leaders in toxic environments. They must be able to identify the root causes of toxicity and develop long-term plans to address them. This might involve restructuring teams, implementing new policies, or advocating for organizational changes. Leaders should be adept at navigating office politics, understanding the underlying power dynamics, and leveraging them to create a more positive work environment.

Mentorship and continuous learning are vital for leadership development. Leaders should seek out mentors who have successfully managed similar situations. Learning from their experiences and insights can provide valuable guidance. Additionally, leaders should invest in their own development through courses, workshops, and reading. Staying updated with the latest management theories and practices equips leaders with a broader toolkit to handle diverse challenges.

Resilience is a key trait for leaders in toxic settings. They must be able to withstand pressure and setbacks without losing their focus or motivation. Building resilience involves developing a strong support network, maintaining a healthy work-life balance, and practicing self-care. Leaders should model these behaviors for their team, demonstrating that it is possible to thrive even in difficult circumstances.

Leaders must also be agents of change. They should advocate for a healthier work culture and be willing to challenge the status quo. This requires courage and a commitment to ethical principles. Leaders should address toxic behaviors head-on, whether they come from peers, superiors, or subordinates. By setting a standard for respect and integrity, leaders can gradually shift the organizational culture towards a more positive and productive state.

In essence, leadership development in toxic environments demands a multifaceted approach. It involves cultivating personal skills, building strong relationships, and strategically navigating the complexities of the workplace. Effective leaders are those who can inspire their teams, manage stress, and drive positive change, even in the most challenging conditions.

Employee Empowerment

In the chaotic landscape of toxic project environments, empowerment of employees stands as a beacon of hope and productivity. The essence of employee empowerment lies in granting team members the authority, resources, and confidence to make decisions and take actions that align with the project's objectives. This empowerment can transform a stifling, micromanaged atmosphere into a dynamic, creative, and motivated workspace.

The first step in fostering employee empowerment is to build a foundation of trust. Trust is not merely given; it is earned through consistent, transparent communication and by demonstrating faith in the team's capabilities. Leaders who trust their employees encourage a sense of ownership and accountability, which in turn fosters a more committed and engaged workforce. Trust can be cultivated by recognizing and valuing the unique contributions of each team member, and by providing a safe space for them to express ideas and concerns without fear of retribution.

Autonomy is another critical component of empowerment. When employees are given the freedom to make decisions about their work, they are more likely to take initiative and innovate. This autonomy should come with clear boundaries and expectations to ensure alignment with project goals. Leaders can facilitate autonomy by setting clear objectives and allowing team members the flexibility to determine the best methods for achieving these goals. This approach not only enhances creativity but also reduces the bottlenecks associated with constant oversight and approval processes.

Equipping employees with the necessary resources and skills is essential for true empowerment. This includes providing access to tools, training, and information that enable them to perform their tasks effectively. Continuous learning opportunities and professional development programs can help employees stay updated with the latest industry trends and technologies, enhancing their confidence and competence. Additionally, fostering a culture of knowledge sharing within the team can promote collective problem-solving and innovation.

Empowerment also involves recognizing and leveraging the strengths of each team member. Leaders should take the time to understand the individual skills and expertise within their team, assigning roles and responsibilities that align with these strengths. This not only maximizes productivity but also boosts morale, as employees feel valued and understood. Regular feedback and constructive criticism can help employees refine their skills and grow professionally.

Effective communication is a cornerstone of employee empowerment. Open, honest, and frequent communication helps in setting expectations, providing feedback, and addressing any issues that arise. Leaders should encourage a two-way dialogue where employees feel heard and valued. This can be achieved through regular team meetings, one-on-one sessions, and informal check-ins. Transparent communication also helps in building trust and ensures that everyone is on the same page regarding project objectives and progress.

The role of a leader in an empowered team shifts from being a directive authority to a supportive guide. Leaders should focus on removing obstacles that hinder employee performance and providing the support needed for success. This may involve advocating for better resources, mediating conflicts, or providing mentorship and guidance. By adopting a servant leadership approach, leaders can inspire their teams to take ownership and drive the project forward with enthusiasm and commitment.

In toxic environments, the ripple effects of employee empowerment can be profound. Empowered employees are more likely to exhibit higher levels of job satisfaction, engagement, and loyalty. They become proactive problem solvers and innovators, contributing to a more positive and productive project environment. The shift from a control-based to an empowerment-based management style can be challenging, but the benefits far outweigh the efforts, leading to sustainable project success and a healthier organizational culture.

Measuring Success

In the labyrinth of managing projects within toxic environments, the ability to measure success becomes a beacon of clarity amid the chaos. The metrics and benchmarks serve not just as indicators of progress but as vital tools to navigate the murky waters of dysfunctional workplaces. The challenge lies in establishing a framework that is both resilient to the toxicity and adaptable to the fluctuating dynamics of the environment.

One of the first steps in measuring success is identifying key performance indicators (KPIs) that align with the project's objectives. In a toxic setting, traditional KPIs may need to be re-evaluated and tailored to reflect the unique challenges faced. For instance, while time and budget adherence remain crucial, additional KPIs such as team morale, communication effectiveness, and conflict resolution efficiency might be necessary. These indicators provide a more holistic view of the project's health and help in addressing the underlying issues that could derail progress.

Data collection in such environments requires a nuanced approach. Surveys and feedback forms must be designed to encourage candid responses without fear of retribution. Anonymity can play a critical role here, allowing team members to voice concerns and highlight issues that might otherwise be suppressed. Regular check-ins and one-on-one meetings can also serve as valuable touchpoints to gather qualitative data, offering insights that numbers alone cannot provide.

Analyzing the collected data involves looking beyond the surface. Patterns and trends can reveal the root causes of recurring problems. For example, frequent delays might not be merely a scheduling issue but could indicate deeper issues such as lack of resources, poor communication, or even burnout. By delving into the 'why' behind the data, project managers can develop targeted strategies to address these underlying causes.

Setting realistic and flexible milestones is another critical aspect. In toxic environments, unexpected obstacles are almost guaranteed. These might range from interpersonal conflicts to abrupt changes in organizational priorities. Therefore, milestones should be designed with a degree of flexibility, allowing for adjustments as the project progresses. This adaptive planning ensures that the project remains on track even when faced with unforeseen challenges.

Celebrating small wins becomes essential in such settings. Recognizing and rewarding achievements, no matter how minor, can boost morale and foster a sense of accomplishment. This positive reinforcement helps to counterbalance the negative aspects of the environment, motivating the team to maintain their efforts and continue striving towards the project's goals.

Effective communication is the linchpin that holds the entire measurement framework together. Transparent, consistent, and open lines of communication ensure that everyone is on the same page. Regular updates, meetings, and reports help in keeping the team informed about progress, setbacks, and any changes in direction. This transparency builds trust, which is often in short supply in toxic environments, and keeps the team aligned with the project's objectives.

In the end, measuring success in toxic environments is not just about hitting targets but about understanding the intricate dynamics at play. It requires a delicate balance of quantitative metrics and qualitative insights, combined with a flexible and adaptive approach. Through careful monitoring, continuous feedback, and a focus on both the tangible and intangible aspects of the project, success becomes not just a goal but a journey of resilience and growth.

www.ingramcontent.com/pod-product-compliance
Lightning Source LLC
Chambersburg PA
CBHW071922210526
45479CB00002B/520